Parish Path
through Advent and Christmastime

Parish Path through Advent and Christmastime

Edited by Mary Ann Simcoe

The following articles originally appeared in *Liturgy 80,* November/December 1982: "Epiphany and the Gift of Time," "A Merry Christmas Bulletin," and "Preaching in Advent: Rethinking the Fulfillment Theme."

 Liturgy Training Publications, 1800 North Hermitage Avenue, Chicago IL 60622-1101; 312/486-7008.

ISBN 0-930467-14-0

Cover art by Suzanne M. Novak
Photos on pages 41, 46, 47, 49 by Regina Kuehn
Photo on page 45 by Mary Ann Simcoe

Contents

Introduction

Mary Ann Simcoe

When we turn the clocks back an hour each fall, the reality of growing nights and shortening days engulfs me. Now I rise in semi-darkness, and when I leave my workplace hours later, I face darkness once again. Night's blackness seems to me banishment, isolation, exile. It is not so much the winter's cold that I long to escape, but the darkness itself. Let me hibernate until daylight returns.

When the day of longest night comes round, is Earth caught in indecision between darkness and light? The makers of our language thought so. *Solstice* means "sun standing still." Though astronomers' charts assure the annual return to the sun, still I hold my breath, my belief, till by my daily routine I know that Earth has chosen daylight's grace again. Only when the city turns on its lights of winter festival and my neighbors hospitably illumine their doorways and windows do I believe that in a few weeks we will not need light of our own making to chase away the long night.

The winter solstice sets the stage for the Christmas festival in our Northern Hemisphere. During the increasing darkness of Advent days the church proclaims: "Cast off deeds of darkness and put on the armor of light" (First Sunday of Advent, cycle A); "Be constantly on the watch! . . . Do not let him come suddenly and catch you asleep" (First Sunday of Advent, cycle B); "What we await are new heavens and a new earth where, according to his promise, the justice of God will reside'' (Second Sunday of Advent, cycle B); ''Take off your robe of mourning and misery; put on the splendor of glory from God forever. . . . For God is leading Israel in joy by the light of his glory, with his mercy and justice for company'' (Second Sunday of Advent, cycle C).

When Earth has finally leaned toward the sun, we proclaim our Light in Christmas festival: ''Upon those who dwelt in the land of gloom a light has shone. . . . They name him Wonder-Counselor, God-Hero, Father-Forever, Prince of Peace'' (Christmas, Mass at Midnight); ''Light dawns for the just; and gladness for the upright of heart'' (Christmas, Mass at Dawn); ''My eyes have witnessed your saving deed, . . . a revealing light to the Gentiles, the glory of your people, Israel'' (Holy Family, cycle B); ''Your light has come, the glory of the Lord shines upon you. . . . Nations shall walk by your light, and kings by your shining radiance'' (Epiphany).

No time for hibernation this! During darkened days the church speaks not of banishment, but glory; not of isolation, but of gathering the human race; not of exile, but of homecoming. To her own, who themselves must choose between darkness and light, she proclaims: Be ready, stay alert! See the signs of God-with-us. Be the sign of God-with-us. The day of the Lord's coming is not fond memory. The day of the Lord is not only in the future. The reign of the Lord is now to shine and be manifest through this church gathered and living Advent-Christmas virtues: heartfelt mercy, kindness, humility, patience, forgiveness, justice, peace.

The History of Advent-Christmastime

We Christians need not be surprised to learn that the origins of the Christmas festival and its weeks of Advent preparation are anchored in nature's cycle of darkness and light. The solstice phenomenon seems to have been the occasion for the date of Christmas. And surely it influenced the selection of scripture and prayer texts for these days. The origins of this phase of the liturgical year are unclear. But we do know this: In 274 the Roman Emperor Aurelian declared December 25 the Feast of the Invincible Sun to mark the triumph of day over night. (By that century's reckoning, December 25 was the calendar date of the winter solstice.) We know this as well: By 336 the Christians of Rome kept their own festival on

December 25 in honor of the birth of Christ, the "sun of righteousness." Perhaps the Roman Christians inaugurated this day to rally against the pagan feast, or added their own reasons for joining the culture's festivity, or were, in popular belief, convinced that the actual date of Christ's birth coincided with the winter solstice—all are hypotheses of liturgical scholars.

The development of Epiphany as the feast of Christ's birth and manifestation in the Eastern churches may have occurred in somewhat similar fashion. The circumstances surrounding the appearance of this commemoration are even less clear than those of Christmas. We do know that by the end of the fourth century the Epiphany celebration was widespread in the Eastern churches. Epiphany's date, January 6, may, like that of Christmas, have shared that of a pagan festival—a festival in honor of the birthday of a god who is born anew and brings on a new age. Epiphany celebrated the birth of the Lord and also the manifestation of his divinity at his baptism and miracle at Cana. The rites of this day included baptism and blessing of water.

These two feasts of Christ's birth eventually came to be kept throughout the Christian world. Adolf Adam describes this in his history of the development of the liturgical year:

> In the second half of the fourth century East and West took over each other's birthday feast of Jesus. While the East celebrated on December 25 not only the birth of Jesus but also the coming of the Magi and reserved January 6 for the commemoration of Jesus' baptism and his miracle at Cana and for the conferral of baptism, the West on January 6 celebrated the Epiphany of the redeemer in connection with the coming of the wise men, the baptism of Jesus and the wedding feast at Cana. . . . J. A. Jungmann puts the thematic difference between the two feasts in this way: "The mystery of the incarnation is the proper subject of them both; but at Christmas we consider chiefly the coming down of the Son of God who became one of the poor children of men, while on Epiphany we direct our attention to this child's divine dignity which already is beginning to manifest itself in the world." (*The Liturgical Year,* Pueblo Publishing Company, 1981. 145-46.)

With their proper emphases, Christmas and Epiphany "frame" what came to be called the twelve days of Christmas (the days from December 26 through January 6). During these days of festival (which, in the United States, may number more or less than 12 because Epiphany is kept on the Sunday from January 2 to January 8), the church treasures the closeness and graciousness of the Lord who reveals himself in our flesh.

The development of Advent, the time of preparation for Christmas, is more difficult to trace than that of any of the seasons the church keeps. Scattered records from the fifth through seventh centuries indicate that an Advent liturgy took shape slowly. In Rome, the Christmas preparation seems at first to have been limited to the last days before the feast itself. The evolution of a weeks-long pre-Christmas season may have come from those areas where Epiphany baptism was customary; as Lent was the final preparation for Easter baptism, the weeks preceding Epiphany appear to have been used similarly. From Spain to Rome, from Gaul to Ravenna the focus of prayer during the pre-Christmas weeks varied from expectation of the Lord's final coming to the incarnation of Christ. In Gaul, "Advent" had a penitential character (probably drawn from prebaptismal practice), but not so in Rome. Local traditions spread from one region to another, and Advent today is marked by this commingling of elements. Although we don violet vestments, it is not with Lent's penitence. We do not sing the Gloria during these days, but neither is this in penitence, but so that at Christmas the *Gloria in excelsis Deo* may seem a new and fresh proclamation. While we sing "Rejoice!" we are not to relax in our joy, but to be vigilant. Advent's mix of focuses—looking toward the end times and recalling the birth of Jesus—has made this a season rich in scripture texts and prayers and unrivaled in folk customs.

Planning the Advent-Christmas Liturgies

Our lives today are barely inconvenienced by darkness and winter cold. We cope well with nature's cycles by the grace of technology, but our darknesses are no less real and our era perhaps more terrible than that of our ancestors in faith. For many the Advent days are frantic and hurried as they keep step with our culture's Christmastime demands. For most of us Christmas touches some memory of childhood wonder and reminds that the once-upon-a-time wonder will never be recaptured. For many more than we realize, our culture's expectation of Christmas togetherness sharply contrasts with the experience of longings unfulfilled or relationships ended; the days of joy become a time of tears choked back or cold cynicism. And for us all there is the communal darkness of our war-torn century, our clutching culture, our selfishness and blindness to injustice.

During the days between darkness and light, the church no longer sings its song against the backdrop of the Roman Feast of the Invincible Sun. But how much we still need this yearly proclamation of the birth of the "sun of righteousness" and manifestation of the Lord. This book's premise is that we, the church, need Advent-Christmastime. We keep these seasons not simply because they are our inheritance. They are our inheritance because in the midst of winter our hearts still long for the light, hope, challenge, promise, glory of these days—and the days to come. The lectionary and sacramentary, the foundations of Advent-Christmas planning and prayer, show us today where our hope lies and how we are to live. We keep the Advent-Christmas rituals, sing these season's songs, make their gestures, retell their stories, because they continue to shape our Christian identity. Liturgists need not turn to rivalry with shopping mall glamour to lure their assemblies into keeping these seasons. They need only unfold, lay open the treasury inherited from those who have gone before us in faith. They need to assure that the telling of this birth in the midst of winter is strong and true. They need place no false demands upon their people, no additional burdens, only the demands of the gospel itself.

The chapters of this book outline the main areas for liturgy planners' attention. Lectionary and sacramentary are the privileged sources which guide our common prayer, and are the first elements to consider. The lively arts which give shape to and embody our prayer come next: gesture, visual art, music. Planners may find the worksheets and background provided in *Groundwork: Planning Liturgical Seasons* (LTP, 1982) helpful companions to preparing Advent-Christmastime with these elements of celebration in mind.

On the Thursdays of Advent the church prays: "Let our lives be honest and holy in this present age, as we wait for the happiness to come when our great God reveals himself in glory." Well might this be the prayer and attitude of those who prepare this season's liturgies. Alongside the glittery falsehood of Christmas commercialism, households also know honesty and holiness in their customs—the honesty of homemade cookies and the scent of fresh evergreen, the holiness of hospitality and a Christmas letter to an old friend. The rites of Advent-Christmastime deserve no less than this kind of truth. Their scriptures and prayers, gestures and songs need only gracious space, truly thoughtful planning, strong local traditions. Then the church can gather in the face of darkness and open itself to receive the light which darkness cannot overcome.

The Lectionary

Eugene LaVerdiere, SSS

Advent

Advent is a proclamation of the Lord's coming as the Son of Man, *the* human being, and as Emmanuel, God-with-us. It is a celebration of God's promise that the Lord will indeed come and a Christian commitment to make ready his way. Its fundamental attitudes are joyous hope, loving trust and unwavering perseverance. Many of Advent's readings refer to events long past and persons associated with Jesus' first coming. They also include some of Israel's finest poetry and exciting selections from the early church's classic collection of letters. Advent's focus, however, is not on the past but on the future. It sees those events and persons as symbols and models for a new advent which stretches before us to the horizon of history, when God's designs for humanity and our deepest aspirations will be fulfilled.

In relation to the New Testament's gospel accounts, cycles A and C are quite homogeneous, with their readings drawn from Matthew and Luke respectively. The same cannot be said for cycle B, whose readings come from John and Luke as well as Mark. It remains true, however, that the three synoptic gospels set the tone for the three cycles. With Matthew we celebrate Advent as missionary Christians who are aware of their roots in Judaism as well as of their religious uniqueness. With Mark we see Advent in the context of our radical commitment to follow Christ, whatever the cost. With Luke our Advent unfolds as a work of the Holy Spirit, reconciling everyone through Jesus, the savior, messiah and Lord of all.

For the first reading, Isaiah is our Advent prophet *par excellence.* To appreciate his poetry as well as the other Advent readings from the Hebrew Scriptures, it is important to realize that these readings do not point exclusively toward a Christian fulfillment. Today as always, they provide religious language for both Jews and Christians, for all whose spirit burns with the fire of God's eternal word.

In our path through the Advent lectionary, we are made very much aware of the theme of promise and fulfillment. This biblical theme is fundamental for Advent, in which we see the present time as a fulfillment with regard to past history and as a promise of future fulfillment. In this our point of reference is always the present, not the past. The New Testament in its time could look back to the Old and see in its pages the promise of what was now fulfilled in its gospel experience. Until that moment, however, that promise remained undisclosed, hidden in God's mystery. Religious Jews of the time could do the same for their synagogue experience. Today we see how the New Testament itself is fulfilled in its daily unfolding, full of surprises as its rich potential is gradually revealed.

In addition to the biblical context, we must be equally aware of the liturgical setting for our readings. It is not enough to interpret the readings in their ancient literary framework. We must now see them as related to one another in the liturgy and as their combined message is brought to bear on the eucharistic celebration and proclamation. In the liturgy, the church brings texts together in a new way. These texts comment on and illumine one another, creatively revealing meaning for our time which these texts do not have when they are considered exclusively in their biblical, literary and theological context.

CYCLE A

In cycle A, the Sundays of Advent are dominated by Matthew's gospel. We begin with a passage from Jesus' discourse on the coming of the Son of Man (Mt 24:37–44), continue with the work and message of John the Baptist (Mt 3:1–12; 11:2–11) and conclude with an account of how

Jesus first entered into the world (Mt 1:18–24). These readings from Matthew have been given a new liturgical context which Matthew could not have imagined. To discover this new order, we have only to read the four gospel readings sequentially. For Christians today who look with hope to the final coming of Christ and who wish to prepare his way (Mt 24:37–44), John the Baptist is an excellent model (3:1–12; 11:2–11) and the account of Jesus' first coming into the world shows how Jesus' final coming will be of God (1:18–24). Such is the Advent gospel for cycle A.

First Sunday

The first Sunday situates us in religious history. Jesus who was born long ago and whose life climaxed in the passion-resurrection will return as Son of Man and Lord. Shall we be among those who go about unconcerned? Or shall we be like the servant faithfully fulfilling our mission when the Son of Man returns? We do not know the time of the Lord's coming. All the more reason for preparedness! (Mt 24:37–44)

It is not easy to express what the Son of Man's coming will mean. How can we speak of things which lie beyond history and transcend human experience? We need images and symbols which point beyond what we see and touch. Poetic verses from Isaiah provide the needed language. As in ages past, we look to the Lord's coming as a day of peace, when all nations will gather at the Lord's dwelling place, a mountain higher than every other. Let swords become plowshares. Let spears become pruning hooks. Let us climb the Lord's mountain, walking in his light (Is 2:1–5). The second reading, a Pauline exhortation, develops the theme of light and applies it to various life contexts (Rom 13:11–14).

Second Sunday

On the second Sunday, John the Baptist and his message help us to grasp our role as we prepare for the Lord's coming (Mt 3:1–12). It is not just a matter of preparing ourselves personally for that coming. Like John we have a mission to others. Called to discipleship, we are called to mission. John's mantle of camel's hair has fallen on our shoulders, and it is we who must now proclaim the proximity of God's kingdom and call everyone to reform. We do this as twentieth century heralds in the desert urgently pleading that the Lord's way be well prepared. As in John's case, there is always a danger that our mission will eclipse the Lord's coming. The one who is coming is more powerful than we are. Therein lies our hope. We are not worthy to carry his sandals. Without John's humble self-appraisal, we are powerless in our mission.

Few if any passages from the Hebrew Scriptures sum up our hopes for Advent and the purpose of our mission better than Isaiah's poetic vision of the reign of Emmanuel. A new shoot will sprout from Jesse's ancient root, a king who will fulfill every hope. The spirit in which he will rule will be that of the Lord himself. Rich in the gifts of God's spirit, he will rule with justice. His reign will reestablish our long lost Eden, a garden of peace and life (Is 11:1–10). A short reading from Paul's letter to the Romans draws our attention to the person of Christ Jesus whose spirit guides us as we turn to the scriptures in pursuit of our mission (Rom 15:4–9).

Third Sunday

On Advent's third Sunday, the gospel again turns to the story of John, his disciples, and their relationship to Jesus (Mt 11:2–11). On the second Sunday, John had announced that someone would come who was far greater than he. On the third, John sends his disciples to inquire of Jesus whether he was the one whose way John had been preparing. Although hope was secure, the manner of its concrete fulfillment was unclear. The same remains true today. Jesus' answer to John's disciples is his answer to us, lest we settle for a false messiah. At the Lord's coming, those who are blind see, the crippled walk in the way of the Lord, the deaf hear his word and the dead rise to a life beyond imagining. The good news is preached to the poor, to those whose only hope is in God.

As on the two previous Sundays, the first reading is taken from the book of Isaiah (35:1–6, 10). As the poet exults in the salvation brought by the Lord's presence, his vision colors all of creation. The desert, the mountains, the rivers and all of animate nature are transformed before his eyes. Like Isaiah and with him, our spirit quickens at the Lord's approach. The same nature which reflects God's presence to us, mirrors our response to him as we sing of the salvation he brings. The Lord's coming, for which we yearn and to which we dedicate our efforts, is celebrated in anticipation. For the human spirit which is attuned to God, the distinction between past, present and future vanishes. So attuned, it is easy to accept the second reading's admonition to be patient (Jas 5:7–10).

Fourth Sunday

We have come to the fourth and climactic Sunday in our Advent celebration according to Matthew. The gospel reading is taken from Matthew's infancy narrative, which approaches Jesus' coming into the world from the point of view of Joseph. In cycles B and C, the point of view is that of Mary. The story of Joseph's quandary with regard to Jesus' human origins highlights the divine origins of the savior. Jesus is really Emmanuel, "God is with us." The gospel helps us to keep our Advent preparations in proper focus. The person whose way we prepare is no mere human being. Our Advent is in view of God's being fully and definitively with us (Mt 1:18–24).

In the first reading, Isaiah speaks to us of the sign which will accompany the Lord's salvation: a virgin shall be with child, bear a son and name him Emmanuel (Is 7:10–14). From earliest times, the church has drawn inspiration from Isaiah's prophetic word and transformed it into a statement of Jesus' identity. Today, with Jesus' life in the distant past, our liturgy turns to the same text to speak of the sign which will accompany the Lord's final coming. The church itself is the virgin with child. On Christmas, when she greets the Lord in anticipation of his coming, she will name him Emmanuel. The second reading, which is taken from the introduction of the letter to the Romans, distinguishes Jesus' human origins from his divine origins and relates his divine sonship to his resurrection (Rom 1:1–7). Paul's gospel becomes our own.

CYCLE B

In cycle B, the basic context of Advent is set on the first two Sundays with readings from Mark's gospel, but since Mark does not dwell on the origins of Jesus, the last two Sundays draw their gospel reading from John and Luke. As in cycle A, the first Sunday situates us with regard to Jesus' future coming as the Son of Man (Mk 13:13–37). On the second Sunday, the gospel is taken from Mark's prologue and develops the role of John the Baptist in preparing the way of the Lord (Mk 1:1–8). The third Sunday again deals with John the Baptist in a composite reading from John's prologue (1:6–8) and the opening of the gospel proper (1:19–28). The season ends with a gospel reading of the annunciation according to Luke (1:26–38), a passage which deals with Jesus' origins in a way quite similar to the corresponding Matthean reading in cycle A: Jesus' life and whole being are of God. As in the other cycles, the best way to grasp the church's intention in assembling these readings for Advent is to read them sequentially.

First Sunday

On the first Sunday we take stock of the times in which we live, and we turn to Mark who helps us shape a Christian attitude toward what appears to be a world reaching its final days. Our task is to prepare for the Lord's coming. We do so attentively, always on our guard, for we do not know the time of his arrival. Our attitude, however, cannot be that of apocalyptic. The end is not yet. We must pursue our mission to others and not be immobilized by fear of the end. Mark's discourse on the final days is not itself an apocalyptic proclamation but a response to apocalyptic (13:13–37). It is very much a message for our time.

The first reading (Is 63:16–17, 19; 64:2–7), with its emphasis on God's fatherly care even as it pleads for his coming in power, prepares us for the gospel reading. God may appear to be distant, but he never ceases to be our Father. In 1 Corinthians 1:3–9 we read of Paul's prayer and encouragement for a community whose factions, turmoil and lack of leadership could easily bring it to think that the end was at hand.

Second Sunday

The second Sunday's gospel introduces John the Baptist as a model for Christians committed to preparing the way of the Lord (Mk 1:1–8). Its most remarkable line, however, is the very first, the title of Mark's entire gospel (1:1) which describes Mark's work as "the beginning of the gospel of Jesus Christ, the Son of God." The second Sunday thus buttresses the theme of the first. When so many think that events indicate the end, Mark boldly affirms that it is but the beginning. We must not forget that the story of the visit to the tomb (Mk 16:1–8) with its proclamation of the resurrection in the midst of all the signs of death is also part of the beginning of the gospel. The life of the church continues to be patterned on the events of its beginning.

The first reading is part of the introduction for Deutero-Isaiah's message of comfort and hope, announcing the Lord's coming through the desert, leading his people to salvation (Is 40:1–5, 9–11). Part of the text was used by the New Testament to spell out the mission of John the Baptist. The second reading (2 Pt 3:8–14), with its insistence that in the Lord's eyes a thousand years is as one day, is particularly appropriate in view of the basic purpose of Mark's gospel. We must not be immobilized by fear of the end. We are needed for the mission. The kingdom must yet be proclaimed to all nations.

Third Sunday

The gospel for the third Sunday is drawn from John's prologue (1:6–8) and the beginning of what is frequently entitled the Book of Signs (1:19–28). As in the other cycles, the liturgy evokes the life and mission of John as an interpretation of our own. The text's focus is on John's identity. He is not *the* prophet. He is not the messiah. As we commit ourselves to the missionary goals of Advent, we must remember that our purpose is to prepare the way of the Lord. Sharing the mission of Jesus, we extend his messianic mission. Sharing the mission of John the Baptist, we prepare minds and hearts for the full and perfect manifestation of the messiah.

The first reading is from Isaiah (61:1–2, 10–11). Like Luke 4:18–19, the liturgy takes verses from Isaiah to summarize the Christian mission. Jesus' mission is now ours as we share his spirit and bring good news to the poor, opening the eyes of the blind and releasing the enslaved. That is why we pray without ceasing and why we rejoice, as Paul enjoins in 1 Thessalonians 5:16–24, the day's second reading.

Fourth Sunday

The gospel reading for the fourth Sunday is Luke's account of the annunciation (1:26–38). With Mary, the church listens to Gabriel's greeting, astounded that such words should be spoken to her. Gabriel continues to speak. Mary's mission, which also articulates the mission of every Christian, is to give life and bring forth the Son of God, the Father's very own life, into the world. There is no way such a mission could be fulfilled through human means. For Mary and for the church, it is made possible by the descent of the Holy Spirit. The annunciation looks forward to Pentecost. Pentecost relives the annunciation. Together with Mary, we commit ourselves to be the servants of the Lord.

In its first reading, the liturgy presents part of the story of David, a servant of the Lord whose mission was to prepare him a suitable dwelling (2 Sm 7:1–5, 8–11, 16). The reading's conclusion announces that David's kingdom would endure forever. Such was the promise which Gabriel repeated to Mary. The second reading, the concluding doxology of Romans (16:25–27), provides a fitting "amen" for our Advent celebration.

CYCLE C

In cycle C, the Sundays of Advent are dominated by Luke's gospel. As in the other cycles, the gospel readings begin with Jesus' discourse on the coming of the Son of Man (Lk 21:25–28, 34–36), continue with the role and preaching of John the Baptist (Lk 3:1–6; 3:10–18) and conclude with a narrative statement on the significance of the child who would be born of Mary (Lk 1:39–45). Mined in various sectors of the Lucan quarry and creatively rearranged in a continuous sequence unknown to Luke, the four readings of cycle C constitute our third Advent gospel.

First Sunday

The first Sunday looks to the end of time and the glorious advent of the Son of Man. It speaks to Christians who know that wars, insurrections, earthquakes, plagues, famines and persecutions, like the destruction of Jerusalem, do not announce the end. Terrible as these may be, they are but days of retribution, times to give witness, moments to be met with patient endurance. It speaks to Christians who live in what the gospel calls "the times of the Gentiles" and who know that the end will not come until those times are fulfilled (Lk 21:5–24).

The signs of the end are not historical but cosmic, signs seen in the heavens, in the sun, the moon and the stars, and on earth, in the roaring of turbulent seas. Luke writes like a poet, stretching minds and language to the limits to speak a faith-reality whose significance is beyond imagining. At the Son of Man's approach in power and glory, the very cosmos will be shaken. The glory of the cosmos will be eclipsed completely and its power reduced to naught by the advent of one in whom creation is fulfilled (Lk 21:25–27).

The advent of the Son of Man marks the time of our deliverance from every enslaving power. As the ultimate hope in which history's yearnings are fulfilled, it requires that we stand erect with heads held high, not fearful and cowering (Lk 21:28). For this we must be free of escapist indulgence and worldly cares. To greet the Son of Man and pass this final test of created life in history, we must pray (Lk 21:34–36), as Jesus urgently pleaded at the Mount of Olives (Lk 22:40, 46) and as we do in the Lord's Prayer (Lk 11:4).

A reading from Jeremiah (33:14–16) prepares us for the gospel's hopeful message. The Lord's promise will be fulfilled. A new son of David will come to rule God's people with justice. Judea and Jerusalem will once again dwell secure. In its liturgical context, Jeremiah's prophecy describes the security of those who will stand before the Son of Man (Lk 21:36).

A reading from Paul (1 Thes 3:12–4:2) exhorts us to the kind of life we must live as we prepare the Lord's coming. Above all we must love one another with hearts blameless and holy before God. Liturgically, Paul's message develops Luke's ethical concern that pleasure and wealth not leave us unprepared for the coming of the Son of Man (Lk 21:34–36).

Second Sunday

With the second Sunday, we turn to John the Baptist, a prophet filled with the Spirit from his mother's womb (Lk 1:15) and the greatest of those born of woman (Lk 7:28). In Luke's gospel and in the liturgy, John is a model for all who prepare the Son of Man's final advent. The word of God came to him at a particular moment of world history, just as it comes to us. Like him, we proclaim a baptism of repentance for the forgiveness of sins. The message of Isaiah (40:3–5) describes our mission no less than his. Raising a herald's voice in the desert, we take up John's cry to clear the way for the Lord's coming, to straighten his path and level the road for the advent of salvation (Lk 3:1–6).

In the first reading, Baruch uses the same images to describe the glory of Jerusalem in its moment of salvation. Liturgically, the reading evokes a vision of paradise when the Son of Man will have come and when we shall walk by the light of God's glory in the company of his mercy and justice (5:1–9).

Paul's prayer fills us with confidence as we pursue our Advent mission. We have promoted the gospel until now. We shall persevere until the day of Christ's harvest, a harvest which he has been ripening within us. To prepare the way of the Lord is to open our lives to receive him (Phil 1:4–6, 8–11).

Third Sunday

The third Sunday continues with an account of John's preaching (Lk 3:10–18). After developing his message to those who gathered to hear him, it clarifies his role with regard to the one whose way he was preparing. Again John's life models that of those who prepare the advent of the Son of Man.

John's message is not abstract. It speaks to each one's condition and responsibilities in life. Those who are well clothed and well nourished must share with the indigent. Tax collectors must be honest. Soldiers must not bully, denounce falsely or exploit the local population to supplement their income. Hearing John's message, many wondered whether he might not be the messiah. John, however, merely prepared the way for one who was conceived by the Holy Spirit (Lk 1:35), for an era in which the good news of the kingdom of God would be proclaimed (Lk 16:16). John baptized in water. The messiah would baptize in Spirit and the fire of Pentecost.

Like John, we must not view our life and work as God's definitive manifestation. Our birth in the kingdom and baptism with the Spirit are but a promise. Our mission is to prepare for the day of its fulfillment, a day of winnowing when the wheat will be separated from the chaff and the chaff committed to burning.

John's message is good news. The Lord's approach is reason to rejoice, and rejoicing is the theme of the first and second readings. We hear it first from Zephaniah. Our enemies have been turned away. The king of Israel, the Lord, a mighty savior, is in our midst. He rejoices over us, and we joyfully sing in his love (3:14–18). We hear it then from Paul: Rejoice. The Lord is near. Banish anxiety. Pray. In Christ Jesus, God's peace watches over us (Phil 4:4–7).

Fourth Sunday

The fourth Sunday brings our Advent journey to a climax. Having modeled our mission on John's, we are now ready for the Spirit's quickening spark.

In the gospel, we follow Mary to the hills of Judah and into Zechariah's house. With Mary we greet Elizabeth and thrill at Elizabeth's welcome, an earthly refrain for Gabriel's heavenly salutation: "Rejoice, O highly favored daughter! The Lord is with you. Blessed are you among women" (Lk 1:28); "Blest are you among women and blest is the fruit of your womb" (Lk 1:42). But who are we that our Lord's mother should come to us? At the approach of the one who was conceived by the Holy Spirit, John stirs with the life of the Spirit in his mother's womb. In our sacramental encounter with the risen Lord, we spring to new life. Consecrated in the womb of history, we are now ready for our prophetic mission to usher in the Christmas which fulfills the promise of Bethlehem. Like John the Baptist, we are consecrated by the very one whose way we prepare (Lk 1:39–45).

Micah's prophecy fixes our sight on the horizon of history, to the coming of a ruler born of human insignificance and eternal greatness, a shepherd who brings peace to all peoples in the name of the Lord, his God (5:1–4).

The letter to the Hebrews spells out the meaning of Jesus' coming. Replacing all other sacrifices with a perfect offering of himself, Jesus Christ transforms our covenant relationships into a new covenant in which we are sanctified once for all (10:5–10). Jesus' coming is a new covenant. With the Spirit of that new covenant, we labor for the Son of Man's definitive Christmas. Such is our Advent life in history. Sharing in the feast of promise, we joyfully proclaim its fulfillment. In sacrament, the fullness of Christmas already is in our midst.

Christmastime

Christmas is a celebration of the birth of Jesus, the firstborn, a savior who is both messiah and Lord. It celebrates the manifestation of God's word of life in human flesh, what this incarnation has meant for us, what it realizes through us, and what it will represent at the Son of Man's coming. Christmas is a celebration of Jesus' life in history, sacrament and glory.

Unlike Advent, whose Sundays show well-ordered movement, the Christmas season stands in quiet awe before Christ's birth, like someone unable to move away from a beautiful painting. Its dynamism is contemplative. Rather than a continuous journey, its readings describe a continual return to a wondrous event whose mystery is inexhaustible. These readings are even the same for all three cycles, save for the gospels of the Sunday after Christmas (Holy Family) and the Sunday after Epiphany (Baptism of the Lord).

Vigil of Christmas

Throughout the Christian world, the vigil of Christmas is all but eclipsed by Christmas Mass at midnight. Wherever the liturgy is celebrated on the afternoon or evening of December 24, however, the vigil Mass marks the formal opening of the Christmas season. Its lessons provide a fitting preparation for the three Masses of Christmas day.

The gospel reading is the first chapter of Matthew's gospel, which includes the genealogy of Jesus the messiah (1:1–17) and the account of how his birth came about (1:18–25). While the purpose of the genealogy may be exciting—it is intended to situate Jesus in the history of Israel—its reading is usually quite dull. Were we familiar with Israelite history, however, the names in that reading would be extremely evocative and the genealogy would make a powerful theological impact on us. So as not to bore the assembly with the good news of Jesus' origins, it might be best to read only those sections which are apt to resonate in popular Christian consciousness and to move on to the story of how Jesus' origins transcended every biblical generation. Jesus was not the son of Joseph. Conceived virginally, he was the Son of God.

As in much of Advent and the Christmas season, the first reading is from Isaiah. With the poet, we sing of Jerusalem's glory. Fulfilling her historic destiny, Jerusalem receives a new name from the Lord, a new identity, the Lord's *Delight* and *Espoused* (62:1–5). For Christians at Christmas, the divine espousal is fulfilled in the birth of Emmanuel. With a Pauline address to the synagogue at Pisidian Antioch, Luke reviews the history of Israel and proclaims the birth of Jesus, a savior for Israel (Acts 13:16–17, 22–25).

Christmas Day

Year after year, we open the day with the beginning of Luke's account of Jesus' birth (2:1–14). In a midnight liturgy, we join Bethlehem's shepherds in nightwatch over their flocks. We hear the Lord's messenger proclaim the good news, a gospel for us and for the whole people, that a savior is born to us, the messiah and Lord. The gospel is proclaimed in both word and symbol. Wrapped in swaddling clothes, the savior is a mortal human being like all of us. Reclined in a manger, his person is nourishment for the life and strength of the flock.

Jesus' birth in Judea's Bethlehem is an event in imperial history. David's heir is born in the city of David as a result of Caesar's decree. His birth is also an event in salvation history. Mary's firstborn is the "first born" from the dead. Finding no room in the earthly house of David, his life is offered in saving sacrifice at the table of the manger. Rising as Lord of all, he inaugurates the eternal Davidic reign.

The midnight liturgy is a keynote liturgy. Its gospel reading continues at dawn, when the shepherds go to Bethlehem, see what the angel had proclaimed, and understand everything they had heard. Glorifying and praising God, they become the first to spread the gospel which they had been the first to receive. For her part, Mary, and the church which she represents, treasures and contemplates the gospel event in her heart (2:15–20).

The daytime liturgy provides a second and entirely new synthesis of the gospel event. John's prologue (1:1–18), based on an ancient hymn which drew deeply from the well of Israel's wisdom, celebrates the divine word made flesh, a word which gives God's very own life, a word which is light and which darkness will never overcome. This word is Jesus Christ, God's only Son, the Father's personal revelation.

All three Christmas Masses turn to Isaiah, the Emmanuel-prophet and poet of salvation, for the first reading. With him we sing of light piercing gloomy darkness and of release from servitude in the birth of a wonderful child who will reign in endless peace and justice from David's throne (9:1–6). We sing of a savior king who fills Jerusalem's deserted streets with new life (62:11–12). We sing of the good news of peace and salvation. The Lord God is indeed our king, a comforting king for all the world to see (52:7–10). At Christmas, Isaiah's hopeful vision is celebrated in fulfillment.

The second readings focus first on the salvation which God offered us in Christ's first manifestation. We must live a holy life as grateful people. Christ sacrificed himself for us, saving us by a baptism of rebirth through the Holy Spirit. We must live in hope, awaiting his full manifestation in glory (Titus 2:11–14; 3:4–7). With the letter to the Hebrews, we then reflect on God's incomparable revelation through his Son, the image and firstborn of the Father, who cleansed us from sin and rose to the Father's right hand (1:1–6).

Holy Family

Sunday in the octave of Christmas celebrates the family which Jesus graced and through which he graced the whole human family. In cycle C, we read the conclusion of Luke's infancy narrative (2:41–52), an episode which reveals the ultimate destiny of Mary's son. Born of the Father, he must return to the Father. This simple story of how Jesus journeyed to Jerusalem, was lost after celebrating the Passover and was found in the Temple on the third day prefigures the gospel's great journey to Jerusalem (9:51–24:53). After celebrating the Passover, Jesus would be lost in the passion to be found risen on the third day, afterwards to ascend to his Father in heaven. The young boy sitting in the midst of the teachers reappears as risen Lord, interpreting the scriptures for the apostolic community.

In cycle B, the gospel tells of Jesus' first journey to Jerusalem to be presented in the temple. Simeon and Anna, living voices of Israel's prophetic tradition, proclaim the meaning of his birth for the deliverance of Jerusalem and the salvation of all peoples. Already the passion looms on the horizon (Lk 2:22–40).

In cycle A, the reading is from the sequel of Matthew's account of the visit of the magi. Like the readings from Luke, it shows how the passion already was inscribed in the events of the incarnation and draws attention to the Gentiles' saving role during Christianity's infancy. Warned by an angel, Joseph takes Jesus and Mary and finds refuge in Egypt to escape Herod's murderous designs. Upon returning, they settle in Galilee at Nazareth due to threatening conditions in Judea. Their flight and return both were according to the scriptures (2:13–15, 19–23).

In all three cycles, the first reading is from Sirach. Imparting wisdom to the young, he urges respect and loving consideration for aging parents and speaks the blessings which come to those who honor their father and comfort their mother (3:2–6, 12–14). An exhortation from Paul's letter to the Colossians, the second reading summarizes the attitudes which Christians in general must have toward one another and applies these to wives, husbands and children in a Christian family (3:12–21). In their liturgical setting, the two readings spell out the qualities of family life in the household of salvation.

Mary, Mother of God

On January 1, the octave of Christmas, we gather for the solemnity of Mary, Mother of God. The feast's close link with Christmas is clear from the gospel, which repeats most of the reading for Christmas Mass at dawn. Again we follow the shepherds to Bethlehem's manger (Lk 2:16–20). This time, however, our attention is directed mainly to Mary, her mother's role in the Christmas event and her religious response to all that had happened.

Fittingly, the reading continues with Luke's brief account of the Christmas octave, the day of Jesus' circumcision, the day on which he was given the name Jesus. The circumcision, however, is barely mentioned and only to introduce the naming event. Jesus' name is his personal word, a proper word inseparable from his identity, a word which expresses his relational self. Like the person of Jesus, the name is of divine origin, given to Mary by the angel who announced his conception (Lk 2:21). Divinely born, Jesus was divinely named.

The first reading is from Numbers. With Aaron, we invoke

the Lord's name, summon his gracious presence and call his peace upon the people (6:22–27). The second reading shows the ancient blessing's fulfillment in the life and prayer of those who are adopted children of God. Within their hearts, the Spirit of the Son, of the one named Jesus, the Son of the Most High (Lk 1:31–32), cries "Abba!" and witnesses to their freedom as heirs (Gal 4:4–7).

Epiphany

Epiphany is one of the major feasts in our Christmas season. Having celebrated Jesus' birth and the conferring of his name, we now celebrate his manifestation. Jesus' birth signals salvation for both Jews and Gentiles, and all can invoke his name. (In some countries, the feast is observed on the Second Sunday after Christmas and displaces that Sunday's liturgy. Other countries retain the traditional observance on January 6.)

The gospel reading tells of the visit of the magi, Gentile astrologers from the East, and how the birth of the royal messiah was revealed to them. Matthew's story presents their coming to Jerusalem, their going to Bethlehem, the homage they offered Mary's child, and their return journey to their homeland. It also describes Herod's disturbance and his plot to find the child with the assistance of the magi, a plot foiled by a divine message communicated to the magi in a dream. In Matthew's telling, it is through the Gentiles that Jerusalem learns of the birth of its king, and it is through these same Gentiles that he escapes Jerusalem's machinations. Here is revelation to and through the Gentiles!

The story's major symbol is a star, a revealing star which rises at Jesus' birth and a guiding star which leads the magi to the newborn messiah. Jesus' birth is attested in the heavens, and its heavenly manifestation guides the religious pilgrim to worship. In ancient times, mariners made their way across the sea and caravaners across the desert with the stars as a guide. So also in the journey to Emmanuel.

The magi bring with them the wealth of nations, gold and frankincense, as announced in Isaiah 60:1–6, a hymn to Jerusalem on whom the Lord's light shines and through whom it enlightens the path of the Gentiles. From all sides, caravans come proclaiming the praises of God. In Matthew, the magi also bring myrrh, a precious ointment used in preparing the dead for burial. The good news of the passion is proclaimed in the gift of the magi. Jesus' passion is not just the tragic fulfillment of Herod's destructive design. It is an anointing, a messianic event in which the king born in Bethlehem is revealed as the Christ.

In the second reading, we reflect on the way God's mysterious plan of salvation, long hidden, is now revealed in Christianity's openness to all peoples, to Jews as expected but to Gentiles as well, co-heirs with the Jews, and beneficiaries of the gospel's promise (Eph 3:2–3, 5–6).

Baptism of the Lord

The Christmas season concludes with a celebration of the Baptism of the Lord on the Sunday after Epiphany (except when Epiphany is kept on a Sunday and that Sunday falls on January 7 or 8). Like the Fourth Sunday of Advent, the feast celebrates the gift of the Spirit, and like that Sunday it both recapitulates the season it concludes and brings us to the threshold of the next.

The gospel reading varies with each cycle as we hear Matthew 3:13–17 (cycle A), Mark 1:7–11 (cycle B) and Luke 3:15–16, 21–22 (cycle C) tell of Jesus' baptism by John the Baptist. Each of these recalls John's testimony that Jesus is greater than he. Jesus' life and mission are consequently not to be measured by his association with John and the nature of John's baptism. In an effort reminiscent of Luke's annunciation account, we hear the evangelists tell of the origins of Jesus' mission in the Spirit of God which descends on him after he comes out of the water. Divine in his conception, Jesus is equally divine in his mission. The Spirit makes Jesus God's beloved Son, the one on whom his favor rests. To dissociate Jesus even further from John, Luke mentions only that the baptism had taken place. Jesus' divine manifestation occurs later while he is at prayer.

The first and second readings are the same in all three cycles. With Isaiah we sing of God's chosen one. Gifted with the Spirit, he establishes God's covenant in suffering service that justice might reign among all nations, that the blind might see and prisoners be released from the darkness of confinement (42:1–4, 6–7). Liturgically, this first reading prepares us for Jesus' baptism and situates it with regard to the baptism of the passion. It also looks to the universal Christian mission, an aspect of the baptism to which Peter returns in a reading from Acts. Jesus' mission sprang from his anointing with God's Spirit after the baptism by John. Risen, that same Jesus is now Lord of all, and those who continue his mission must pursue it in openness to all nations (10:34–38). Our Christmas contemplation has fired us for our mission to the ends of the earth.

The Sacramentary

Peter J. Scagnelli

The path through the sacramentary's Advent and Christmastime offerings is a journey through territory lovingly preserved and thoughtfully enriched, a pilgrimage of faith through the church's rich heritage of traditions and texts. Celebrants and planners will want to prepare early, prayerfully and well so that these days may speak to their communities with all the comfort and challenge that the centuries have woven into these specially loved seasons.

As in all aspects of liturgical planning, the use of the sacramentary is a delicate art, an exercise in balance: everything is to be done thoughtfully, reverently, pastorally. The Second Vatican Council has provided us with well-crafted tools and resources. The challenge is to become artists who are faithful to the centuries-old heritage and sensitive to the new-as-today context in which the rites are celebrated. We are to explore and root the community in traditions that have spoken to generations and to discover and refine the words and gestures that will become the traditions of tomorrow.

Therefore, the purpose of these notes is not to offer a vast and ever-changing array of fresh "creations" custom-tailored to every element of every week's liturgy. Rather, specific suggestions are made within a general overview of the season under consideration. The notes should be read with reference to the other sections of this path book, since the words and gestures of the sacramentary, however important, are part of a much broader context of atmosphere, attitude and environment. In liturgical planning as much emphasis (if not more) ought to be given to what should *not* change from week to week as to what should! This is a different approach from that presented in many popular "pastoral aids," but seems to be more consistent with the best insights of recent studies in ritual and more faithful to the spirit of Vatican II's liturgical books.

Gimmickry will always be out of place. The "brand new" this year (implied: "to be thrown away next year") is never presumed to be the first or best choice in liturgical planning. We owe it to our ancestors in faith, and even more to our children and our children's children, to receive reverently and gratefully the gift of the past, to implement it carefully and to enhance it intelligently in the present, so that our posterity will be able to carry it thankfully into the future.

Advent

> The season of Advent has a two-fold character. It is a time of preparation for Christmas when the first coming of God's Son to us is recalled. It is also a season when minds are directed by this memorial to Christ's second coming at the end of time. It is thus a season of joyful and spiritual expectation. (*General Norms for the Liturgical Year and the Calendar,* #39)

Perhaps there has never been a time in the church's history when this "two-fold character" has been kept in balance, but with the reformed liturgical books, there has probably never been a better time to try! The sacramentary reminds us that the focus is on the eschatological through December 16, and the liturgy urges us to look toward the second coming of Christ. From December 17 through 24 the daily propers prepare us more directly for the celebration of Christmas. Fidelity to this twofold dimension should guide our careful choices as we prepare to celebrate this season. Celebrants and planners will want to examine the readings and notes for all the Sundays of Advent and begin, as well, to look beyond to Christmas, Epiphany and the Baptism of the Lord. Such an "overview" approach to seasonal planning can help ensure the consistency and contrast that allow verbal and visual, musical and ritual elements to blend into the brief and peaceful, but powerfully significant, preparation Advent is meant to be.

General Atmosphere

Advent's general atmosphere could be described thus: Joyful expectation. Anticipation. The special urgency animating those who know that a time of new beginnings is at hand. The quiet confidence of children assured of their parents' love. Grace. Simplicity. Serenity. The cleanliness of a house reverently set in order for the coming of one who is both cherished friend and awesome judge.

The visual and aural environment of worship can speak of a new season before the liturgy even begins! No doubt the Advent wreath (candles large enough to be seen and to last) will be visible to all who enter. The sparseness of ornamentation and the elimination of useless sanctuary clutter can signal a new seriousness of purpose. This quiet austerity might be enhanced by a generous but tasteful use of seasonal color in vesture, tapestry and lectionary cover. All music will have been carefully selected (and taught) in advance. Seasonal responsorial psalm and alleluia as well as new eucharistic acclamations should make their debut now and continue throughout the season (perhaps right into Christmastime). One ancient custom tones down the visual environment by eliminating all floral arrangements (since these will be so much in evidence during the Christmas season), and current legislation still eliminates instrumental music "except as needed to sustain singing" on all but the third ("Gaudete") Sunday and December 8 (*Instruction on Sacred Music,* May 3, 1967, #66).

Introductory Rites

Careful thought should be given to the beginning of the liturgies in this season of beginnings. A quiet procession through a dimly lit church to an a cappella chanting of a traditional Advent tune might well mark the opening (and closing) of Advent's Masses. "O come, O come, Emmanuel," "Creator of the stars," *"Rorate coeli,"* and other gems from the tradition are, or ought to become again, signal sounds of the Advent observance.

The sacramentary provides no ceremony or prayer for the blessing and lighting of the Advent wreath. Popular aids have supplied such elements, but many of these, although sometimes beautiful and scriptural, are verbose and tend to overemphasize this one element of Advent's liturgy. One possible alternative might be this set of simple and scriptural invocations offered as a "light service" in the *Lutheran Book of Worship:*

Cantor or presider:	The Spirit and the church cry out:
All:	Come, Lord Jesus!
Cantor or presider:	All those who await his appearance pray:
All:	Come, Lord Jesus!
Cantor or presider:	The whole creation pleads:
All:	Come, Lord Jesus!

These could be chanted, perhaps using a melody that will be known already from singing the general intercessions. The lighting, the invocations (with uplifted hands?) and a profound bow might be an appropriate and simple beginning.

The second set of invocations given for form C of the penitential rite is perfectly suited to the dual focus of Advent and might well be repeated on all four Sundays:

> Lord Jesus, you came to gather the nations into the peace of God's kingdom: Lord, have mercy.
>
> You come in word and sacrament to strengthen us in holiness: Christ, have mercy.
>
> You will come in glory with salvation for your people: Lord, have mercy.

Consider, however, the ways in which the words and gestures around the wreath each Sunday might replace the penitential rite and conclude with a sung Kyrie.

The opening prayer should be selected carefully, since the alternatives do not always seem to respect the division of the season noted above. Here is an outline of choices that may be helpful:

- Sunday I: Either is suitable. The first form echoes more the theme of the second coming; the second speaks more directly of light (and may be more appropriate in year C: "Hold your heads high!").

- Sunday II: Both prayers echo the gospel selections in praying that all impediments to welcoming Christ be removed. The first form mentions Christ's coming in glory; the second speaks of the "day of salvation" and seems more suited to the latter part of Advent.
- Sunday III: The first form is clearly Christmas oriented; the second mentions the second coming and reflects the gospels' "change your heart!" call (especially appropriate in year C).
- Sunday IV: Both opening prayers harmonize well with the predominant Marian flavor of this Sunday. The first opening prayer presents the angel's message and the Son's coming and, as the old Angelus collect, deserves to be heard, if not here, then perhaps at the conclusion of the general intercessions. The second form mentions explicitly the Word taking flesh and the virgin's life at the service of the Father's plan.

General Intercessions

The Advent intercessions in the back of the sacramentary are a model of universality and conciseness. Local compositions should be patterned on this. Perhaps, as the sacramentary does for the preface, two forms might be prepared for the general intercessions: one for the "eschatological" part of Advent (until December 17), an alternate form for the latter part. There is no rule that the general intercessions need be composed freshly each week! Our Eastern friends have used the same litany for centuries, while recent Episcopalian and Lutheran revisions provide a limited number of well-written suggestions. These sources might be consulted and some time-honored intercessions incorporated into local compositions:

> For the holy church of God: that it may be filled with truth and love, and be found without fault at the day of Christ's coming: we cry out to the Lord. Come, Lord Jesus!
>
> For those in positions of public trust: that, heeding the timeless prophetic call, they may serve justice and promote human dignity: we cry out to the Lord. Come, Lord Jesus!

For the forgiveness of our sins, and the grace of the Holy Spirit to reform our lives according to the gospel: we cry out to the Lord. Come, Lord Jesus!

Poetic language with strong images can be most relevant, for it speaks directly to every personal situation. Perhaps a few "general" intercessions could be repeated week by week, with one or two timely intercessions inserted weekly, the invitation and concluding collect remaining fixed (or even memorized!). Remember, too, the possibility of chanting a seasonal (unchanging) response, perhaps the same as at the candle lighting: "Come, Lord Jesus!"

Eucharistic Prayer and Communion Rite

Advent I is the preface prescribed until December 17, although the (understandable) temptation will be to change to Advent II early on, when the preaching of John the Baptist is recounted so forcefully. Form B of the memorial acclamation ("Lord Jesus, come in glory!") would be a good choice for the entirety of Advent-Christmastime. Reconciliation II is a eucharistic prayer which speaks beautifully of the Lord's messianic mission:

> God of power and might,
> we praise you through your Son, Jesus Christ,
> who comes in your name:
> he is the word that brings salvation,
> he is the hand you stretch out to sinners,
> he is the way that leads to your peace.

This prayer, if heard throughout the season, might become part of the community's in-memory prayer life, and be a welcome alternative to the oft-heard eucharistic prayers II and III.

Presiders will want to choose one introduction to the Lord's Prayer (ideal: "for the coming of the kingdom") and stay with this until the Baptism of the Lord ("Jesus taught us to call God our Father . . ."). If any elaboration of the communion invitation is thought helpful, remember the beautiful invitatories from the liturgy of the hours:

> This is the Lamb of God who takes away the sins of the world:
> the King who is to come.
> Happy are those who are called to his supper.

This is the Lamb of God who takes away the sins
of the world:
the Lord who is near at hand.
Happy are those who are called to his supper.

Concluding Rites

The entrance pattern might well be repeated: quiet, contemplative, serious, anticipatory. A beautiful solemn blessing is offered for Advent and (contrary to the suggestion in some American editions of the sacramentary) could be repeated (memorized and sung?) throughout Advent. A special dismissal might set a good "going forth" tone: "Let us go forth in peace to prepare the way of the Lord." (Latter part of Advent: "The Lord is at hand: let us go forth in his peace.") And then, a cappella chant or silence.

December 8: Immaculate Conception of the Blessed Virgin Mary

Planners and presiders will want to take special care to let this solemnity speak its powerful message gently and in harmony with the dominant context of Advent. Let the atmosphere of anticipation prevail; it is still Advent! Entrance and candle lighting, greeting and penitential rite can remain the same. Focus attention on the solemnity with a brief introduction, which might well include a succinct summary of this doctrine (still popularly confused with the virginal conception of Jesus). A possible model:

> In the midst of Advent we honor the Virgin Mary in her immaculate conception, and by this title we invoke her as special patroness of our nation.
>
> Praising our Father who kept her sinless from the first instant of her life, and who in his love forgives, let us humbly acknowledge our sins.

Floral arrangements, a preview of the Christmas Gloria perhaps, and instrumental music might highlight the feast, while the acclamations and chants still echo the season. The general intercessions can reflect our Advent longing and our nation's needs as we honor our patroness. The first or third eucharistic prayer with the Advent acclamations might provide a nice balance between solemnity and season, as would the solemn blessing for feasts of our Lady with the Advent dismissal and exit.

Christmastime

General Atmosphere

A rapid succession of feasts helps us to view the mystery of the incarnation from a variety of perspectives. Establish a general pattern of celebration and then let the various feasts dictate special variations. The entrance procession will almost always feature cross and candles throughout the season, but festive banners might denote the changing feasts. Incense will certainly be added on Christmas and Epiphany and perhaps a large vessel of water on the feast of the Lord's Baptism. Form C of the penitential rite has invocations (iii) specifically appropriate for the entire season:

> Lord Jesus, you are mighty God and prince of peace: Lord, have mercy.
>
> Lord Jesus, you are Son of God and Son of Mary: Christ, have mercy.
>
> Lord Jesus, you are Word made flesh and splendor of the Father: Lord, have mercy.

The Gloria will resound again on every feast. The procession with the gospel book might be graced with incense and lights, as might the procession of the gifts during this season. There is no rule against the chanting of the scripture readings. In fact, one publisher provides a rather elaborate version (GIA's *Chants for the Readings,* Joseph T. Kush). Saint Meinrad's Archabbey has prepared selected gospels in the old "solemn tone," and the new Episcopalian altar book repeats the rules and models for chanting found in the old *Liber.* A new psalm and alleluia might blend with the continuing use of Advent's Sanctus, memorial acclamation, and amen to bring both a special sound and continuity. Presiders may want to choose a new introduction to the Lord's Prayer ("Jesus taught us to call God our Father . . .") and a communion invitation ('This is the Lamb of God, the saving Lord who has appeared among us. Happy are those . . .'') and continue these until the Lord's Baptism.

Flowers and candles are time-honored ways of adding prominence to certain aspects of the worship environment. Various feasts will dictate varying arrangements. Lectern, altar and crèche will be emphasized for Christmas through Epiphany. Then the font will assume prominence for the Baptism of the Lord. With general patterns and invariable selections made, presiders and planners are ready to look at individual feasts and to consider appropriate variations. As with Advent planning, this approach presumes a familiarity with the lectionary and reference to the other sections of this book.

Vigil of Christmas

Popular American usage (with emphasis on practicality) has begun to make this a ''family celebration.'' Another approach to the vigil Mass might begin by noting that the Roman *Ordo* extols the practice of celebrating the office of readings at some time during this night. Perhaps this could be combined with the vigil Mass to make Christmas Eve a real vigil and a setting of the Christmastime stage. Some parishes have begun such a service by candlelight; the presider, vested in a cope, begins with a simple greeting and the alternative vigil collect (''we keep vigil for the dawn of salvation''). Then the reading from Isaiah and Leo's Christmas sermon (both from the office of readings) with ''Sion, sing'' or another chant intervening. Finally, the ancient Christmas martyrology (available from Liturgy Training Publications) is chanted, after which all the lights in the church are lit and the *''Adeste fideles''* begins the vigil Mass proper. The first form of the opening prayer, hailing Christ as redeemer even as we remind ourselves of his second coming as judge, prepares us for the readings of the vigil Mass itself.

If four pillar candles served for the Advent wreath, perhaps four white candles of the same size and style might brighten the crèche, which, of course, must never obscure, dwarf or outshine the central focus on the altar. A set of invocations similar to those sung during Advent could serve as a form of blessing (or an introduction to a more elaborate blessing):

Cantor or presider:	The people who walked in darkness have seen a great light:
All:	Come, let us worship the Lord! *(or:* O come, let us adore him!)
Cantor or presider:	For to us a child is born, to us a Son is given:
All:	Come, let us worship the Lord!
Cantor or presider:	And the Word was made flesh and dwelt among us:
All:	Come, let us worship the Lord!

At this Mass and the midnight Mass, Christmas I seems the best preface choice and the first eucharistic prayer has special inserts.

Midnight Mass

Midnight Mass is generally preceded by some form of choir program. Again, the Proclamation of Christmas (martyrology), clipped into a handsomely bound book, would be a fitting conclusion. It could be sung by candlelight from a place close to the crèche. Then, with the church fully illuminated, choir and congregation caroling full-voice, the ritual incensing of altar, crèche and assembly might provide a festal introductory rite. After such a prelude and extended introductory rite (including, of course, the Gloria), the first form of the opening prayer, ancient and succinct, is probably the better choice. A gospel procession with lights and incense, and the solemn chanting of the beloved Lucan nativity account, could be the splendid climax of the liturgy of the word. The solemn blessing should be a part of all the Christmas Masses: chanting this and the dismissal would be a good introduction to a full-voiced, familiar recessional, followed perhaps by a choral postlude.

Mass at Dawn

Planners and presiders might well let this early Mass be what it seems always to have been: a more quiet and contemplative extension of the church's reflection on the mystery we so gloriously welcomed the night before. The second form of the opening prayer expresses this spirit, and quiet need not mean dull: a cappella singing of carols and acclamations should certainly be part of this early morning prayer. Note Christmas prefaces II and III ("we recognize the revelation of God's love" in "the dawning of new light").

Mass of the Day

The lectionary permits the use of the Lucan gospel at these Masses, but surely the Johannine prologue is too beautiful not to be proclaimed (even chanted)! If this Mass is "family oriented" (better this Mass than the vigil Mass!), then perhaps a brief homily might be followed by a similarly brief nativity pageant by the children. Greater-than-normal crowds provide a temptation for some homilists to bemoan the "Christmas-Easter only" situation and to berate the perpetrators of it—thereby confirming the minimally attached in their decision to avoid such harangues on a weekly basis. Better to presume the best: relatives from out-of-town, spouses from other churches, friends of no special commitment have swelled our numbers today (see Appendix)! And possibly a marginal Catholic hoping to be fed with a brief homily that is simple and real might be drawn back "home" to regular worship celebrated reverently and well.

The first opening prayer is the ancient incarnation collect. With inclusive language it could serve at this Mass or as the concluding collect at the general intercessions throughout the season. The rubrics call for a genuflection today during the creed. An unannounced bop-up-and-down by the presider will hardly invite the assembly's participation or make them sensitive to the reverence the rubric is trying to convey. Perhaps a brief introduction is in order: "Today in our profession of faith, thanking God for making our humanity his own in the wonder of the incarnation, we genuflect in reverence when we proclaim the awesome mystery!"

Holy Family

The family and our Christian hopes for it in a troubled world are, realistically, the social dimension of this rather recent addition to the calendar. Popular aids promote and provide "family blessings," but realism and sensitivity seem to urge an avoidance of marriage vow renewals (which many of these popular forms often take). Better a family blessing that includes single parents (and so involves children who may grieve, at this time of the year above all others, the brokenness of their family lives) and the elderly or widowed who may be present with their children and grandchildren.

The second opening prayer speaks of "the value of family life," and Christmas preface II praises the Christ who is "one like us" and who "restores unity." The eucharistic prayers for Masses with children might be appropriate today, and prayer over the people, #7, seems a good choice.

January 1: Solemnity of Mary, Mother of God

This is the World Day of Prayer for Peace and New Year's Day of course, but the primary focus of the season (the Lord's coming, incarnation, manifestation) is best served by honoring Mary as the Roman church did in its earliest days and does now in the revised calendar. Themes of peace and blessings on the New Year could be part of the general intercessions, which might well conclude with the collect from the votive Mass for the beginning of the civil year (#24, back of sacramentary), and there is a solemn blessing, #3, for today as well. On New Year's Eve, some places hold a vigil for which the Episcopalian *Book of Occasional Services* might supplement our liturgy of the hours, and at which the *Te Deum* ("Holy God we praise thy name") is traditional. In all, today is the continuation and reiteration of Christmas joy. The liturgy should still look and sound like Christmas. As with Christmas greetings, so with New Year's best wishes: these might be most appropriately conveyed at the conclusion of Mass before the solemn blessing for the New Year.

Epiphany of Our Lord

Gold and incense, flowers, candles, the best and brightest of the parish's vesture, vessels, visuals should help this feast proclaim in ways beyond words the radiant splendor of the king whom Gentiles come to adore. The first form of the opening prayer speaks of our faith-guided journey to the Lord pointed out by the star. This day was traditionally associated with the proclamation of the year's "movable feasts" and might be an appropriate time to ritualize the sometimes pedestrian task of distributing parish calendars (see Appendix). Let the smoking censer be near at hand for gospel procession, gift procession, and—for the last time—honoring the crèche. Remember the special Epiphany preface, Roman canon inserts, and solemn blessing.

Baptism of the Lord

The Christmas season extends to this feast in a transitional way: our reflection is being directed toward the manifestation of the adult Christ about to embark on his public ministry. It is no longer Christmas day, but the incarnation is still to the fore as we begin the return to Ordinary Time. The honored place held by the crèche should be occupied by the font today, and water might replace incense as the primary visual and sensory experience. The rite of sprinkling could take place at all celebrations today either as a conclusion to the opening rites or after the celebration of infant baptisms. The vessel should be of appropriate size and material, and evergreen branches work very well for sprinkling. The first form is the better opening prayer and the general intercessions might include those involved in the parish catechumenate since the upcoming lenten season will focus so intensely on their faith journey to the paschal font. There is a special preface for today; although the fourth eucharistic prayer has its own preface, it certainly seems appropriate after the readings and preface of the day. Let the Christmas acclamations (and the Gloria) be heard once more, especially to make the transition to Ordinary Time more evident next week. No solemn blessing is provided, but planners might look at form D of the blessing from the baptismal rite or at prayers over the people #9 and #20.

Prayerful and reverent preparation for this gentle but powerful part of the liturgical year can help people lift up their hearts and open their spirits to the God who touches our lives in these sacred mysteries. Well-planned and celebrated, the Advent-Christmas season can quietly but surely prepare us for our later entry into the intensity of Lent-Triduum-Paschaltime, the central focus of the liturgical year, the saving passover of the Word-made-flesh.

Environment and Art

Regina Kuehn

When you visit a church you can immediately tell by the hymns and by the environment if that church has its theology on the right track. This is particularly true during Advent and Christmas when the practices of our popular culture and piety and those of the church coincide.

In itself, the integration of the civic and the Christian calendars (a rare occurrence) would be a joyful event, if it weren't for the inherent danger to Christians who too readily tag along on sentimental concepts offered by the commercial community and its gullible consumers. A close look reveals that there actually exists a clash rather than an integration and that most of us readily or conveniently contribute to it.

For the Christian, Advent-Christmastime is—or ought to be—of an other kind. It is therefore of absolute necessity for all those who plan the environment for these seasons to (1) ask each other what constitutes this "other kind" of observance, (2) take the time to formulate each year anew the true nature of the seasons and (3) talk about the consequences, lest we lose our Christian festal identity.

Advent and Christmas belong together and should be planned as a unit. The whole of the incarnation is not exhausted by the nativity: the great feasts of the Epiphany and the Baptism of the Lord are vital manifestations of Christ's power and mission. The Advent-Christmas season is closely related to

Easter because "on Christmas he already began to die" (Rahner). Therefore, the celebration of his birth must be linked to the paschal mystery. Every Christ-feast is the celebration of suffering, dying and rising. Every Christian feast is a celebration of our redemption, a feast of the second Adam, our savior.

The original gospel of the incarnation is the prologue of St. John: "In the beginning was the Word." You notice no nostalgia, no sweet nativity scene. Liturgy does not encase God in a human body, but tells us how this one child is connected to our redemption, that he is the same Lord whom we celebrate on Easter.

The season begins with eschatology (the second coming of our redeemer as judge, and receiving him upon his glorious arrival in his city) and ends with an unabashed celebration of a historical event, the incarnation.

Liturgy does not deal with abstract problems, but with the real life of a community. The key question to the community then would be: Between the incarnation and the second coming of Jesus, are *we* the advent of the Lord in the world today? Are *we* the bearers of the kingdom in the sense that we are examples of peace in these days torn apart by hunger, strife and injustice? Do we ponder the meaning of our lives, the meaning of history, of humanity, of our family in respect to our salvation?

Advent

Advent has a metabolism all its own. One definition of that word calls it "the sum of the processes concerned with the maintenance of living cells." When I came upon this description in a totally different context, it immediately conjured up the idea of liturgy planning at its best. What a perfect image: the sum of our liturgical efforts keeping all of us spiritually alive!

The Advent metabolism is special. It is so sensitive and finely tuned that even the slightest unbalance may do us harm. For planners involved in creating the environment it might be best to practice great restraint and not to rush into *doing* things, the worst of which would be to "deck" the church for Advent with a "total look" similar to that created by commercial centers.

A Time for Tradition

After reestablishing our theological directions as suggested above, it might be of benefit to observe and put down on paper the living and quietly pulsating mood of Advent in our families, in our (ethnic) communities, in our parish church.

The emphasis here should be on preserving and protecting what is almost lost, rather than creating something new. The danger is real that Christians will abandon the season altogether, and take their cues from department stores rather than from the liturgy. Thus we will eventually miss not only Advent, but the full impact of Christmas as well, because we do not allow ourselves to be prepared for it.

How can environment and art help? First of all by omitting or eliminating everything that has to be labeled as "cute, sweet, darling, adorable," etc. In view of the above considerations, planning, for example, a birthday party for baby Jesus with a cake will not quite do as adult fare. On the constructive side we should plan everything with simple elegance and great dignity *sub specie aeternitatis,* in view of eternity, which means, eschatologically.

The book containing the readings of Isaiah, the prophet of Advent, and the subsequent stories of our salvation, should be carried and presented as if our life depended on it—which it does! The lectionary could receive a decorative cover. Of course, you can purchase such covers, but it would be much more attractive to make one yourself, or rather two—one for the Sunday readings and one for the weekly lectionary. A heavy, coarse linen holds up well. Royal purple looks excellent when a symbol of contrasting color is hand appliquéed, for example, the "Shoot of David," or any other image taken from the very readings that are being proclaimed. Advent would well justify a fine gold cording, outlining the symbol, giving us a foretaste of the Christmas feast.

The vestments are garments worn by contemporary men and women for the sake of a modern assembly, and should, therefore, reflect our present taste in color, cut and material. Once in a while, such as on the feast of St. Nicholas, or on the days of the "O" antiphons, we might want to bring out one of our time-honored, beautiful vestments. During a season when we concentrate on the roots of Christ's family and on our own roots and traditions, such an occasional gesture will allow us to reflect on our strength: throughout the many changes in style and expression and attitudes the church has been truly "traditional," meaning that she has loyally and actively handed down the essentials of faith for us to recognize, to accept and to label with an imprint of our own time.

The wreath is probably the strongest Advent symbol, if we permit it to be strong. Parishes which place an Advent wreath

in an insignificant corner, flat on a table, cannot expect to reap as much of a spiritual harvest from the mere sight or from the rites surrounding this sacramental as do those parishes who plan more creatively.

A large wreath looks splendid when suspended from the ceiling, with candles of adequate size sitting straight and secure. A wreath held up by a strong wrought-iron stand could be moved to the focal point for special services. Homemade arrangements of metal or wooden loops to hold candles and pine branches often turn out very well. Let the engineers in your parish come up with a good idea. There is no need for purple and pink candles; four natural-colored candles are perfect. The symbol of light overcoming darkness and that of the circle—sign of eternal hope—must remain prominent and uncluttered.

In one parish church the large Easter candle holder was placed in the middle of the aisle—right among the people. It supported a magnificent large wreath, weighted down by four short, plump candles. From the position of each of these candles flowed an array of good-quality ribbons in different shades of royal purple, gracefully touching the ground. The very place of the wreath was marked by a large, round, decorative straw mat, thus emphasizing the shape of the circle even more. What a perfect rendering of the *General Norms for the Liturgical Year* which pronounce Advent to be "a season of joyful spiritual expectation"!

Banners are a challenge. If you decide to make new ones, design them without any words, with the possible exception of symbolic words. Most fitting would be *maranatha,* which is Aramaic, the language which Jesus spoke, and means, "Come, Lord, come!" It is an imperative, an invocation that was used already in the liturgy of the earliest church, along with words such as *amen, alleluia* and *hosannah.* In fact, the earliest instructions on the eucharistic prayer of thanksgivng *(Didache,* chapter 10) conclude with the following "Advent" words: "If any are holy—let them come. If any are not holy—let them repent. Maranatha! Amen."

Just for creating atmosphere, long banners of royal purple cloth have a stunning effect when finely tailored and hung well. Large, unadorned wreaths may hang vertically in front of them. The scriptural readings invite themes such as the "Gate of Justice," or Jesus as the "Emmanuel." During the last part of Advent, when we concentrate on the birth in Bethlehem (a reverse octave, if you wish), the "O" antiphons and the genealogy of Christ are favorite themes. Symbols may be attached to banners, or hung from a tree, or sewn to the skirt of the parish Christmas tree.

Christmastime

Christmas is the unabashed feast. And how well we know how to celebrate a feast! It is the festival of fulfilled hopes, yes, but only in the sense that this fulfillment, by its very nature, initiates a new beginning. It opens a new cycle: the crib, the baptism, the teaching, the cross, the tomb and the resurrection, the birth into a new life. All this is symbolized in the one child.

Theoretically we know all this. Yet, when we look at the decor of our churches, we realize that this thought pattern is almost totally blocked out. The concentration is on the nativity, as it ought to be, but with hardly a visual reference to future messianic events and to his final coming in glory. This situation has grown into a real problem, spiritual naiveté, that makes a baby feast out of the nativity and pretends that all our efforts are crowned and over with on Christmas day, or at best on the feast of the Epiphany. Again, we are influenced by the commercial dictate which has no more use for Christmas on the morning after.

The Challenge

How do we who care about environment and art establish and defend a style which does not yet exist and which will, at first, be rather unpopular?

Musicians have an easier task: looking through the lyrics of Christmas hymns we frequently find the entire salvation dynamic expressed in a few words, so that within minutes we learn the whole framework of Christ's messianic mission. Let's take, for example, the beginning lines of a traditional Christmas hymn to Mary: "She will show us the promised one":

At Nazareth she heard the voice . . .
At Bethlehem she bore her son . . .
At Cana when the wine ran out . . .
At Golgotha she felt the pain . . .
At Easter when she heard the news . . .
She showed to us the promised one.

It is not that the scriptural texts of the Christmas-Epiphany season do not provide us with ample material. The problem is that visually we don't quite dare to make the jump.

In my own parish church a large group of women has made two huge, very elegant angel banners. Both figures are serene, their faces sincere, their eyes are fixed on the distant future. One is carrying the lamb, the other one a crown—heavenly spirits foreseeing and predicting by their symbols the future of the messiah. There are quite a number of parishioners who insist that these banners have nothing to do with Christmas.

We had a similar experience with *Chrismons* (though they traditionally enjoy a wider acceptance) when we hung them on our large parish Christmas tree. (Chrismons are Christmonograms, or symbols of Christ, such as the Chi-Rho or the cross in any of its many shapes.) They can be used in a variety of decorative and devotional ways. Hung on the Christmas tree they permit us, with one glance, an understanding that his death is the reason for the birth we celebrate. Having read an invitation and instruction in the bulletin, skillful parishioners responded generously by making beautiful Chrismons, but not without criticism by a few that crosses at Christmastime were "morbid."

If your parish encourages the use of *luminarias* (prepared by placing sand and plumber's candles in paper bags and setting them outdoors to light a path to the entrance of our homes), you might find the same tension. It is a lovely custom to light the way for the Christmas child, inviting him to come into our homes. The implication, though, if you care to explain it to your parishioners, is uncomfortable: once he has come into your home, he will not go away, like a welcome house guest who becomes a burden and a responsibility after a few days. That is the true symbolism of the *luminarias.* When the candles have disappeared in the sand, *he is still there;* he makes demands on us and we have to stick it out with him

until the end times. Our conscience will not permit him to go away, once we really have invited him.

Banners presenting the flight into Egypt have the same tension, especially at a time when fearful flight has become a worldwide political epidemic. It is uncomfortable to think and to depict that this child is still being persecuted daily in all of human flesh. It is easier to sing lullabies and to create images of the infant than to depict the massacre of the Holy Innocents, Christ's first martyrs, and symbols of all the innocent victims of power and fear, Jews and Christians and all the earth's tribes.

All of us responsible for creating the atmosphere have the obligation to show in attitude and in design that "this Child is King forever in judgment and in justice." Otherwise we only tell part of the story.

The liturgical texts of Christmas make it almost impossible to escape this tension—and still we try to do it and slip comfortably away. To the truly creative artists among those reading this chapter, I propose a challenge: venture into a pictorial interpretation of such Christmas concepts as: "This Child is called Father-Forever," or a paradox such as the "Wonder-Counselor, the God-Hero" being announced to the lowliest group of people, the shepherds. The texts are filled with great images; compared with these images, banners proclaiming things like "Noel" are empty and powerless.

There are simple ways, though, which can be accomplished by simple means once the understanding and the desire have been raised among the planners. The Word that became flesh could be acknowledged by a most festive cover for the lectionary, emphasizing the biblical promise: by God becoming flesh, man and woman can become like God, holy and with life forever. The parchment often used for the proclamation of Christmas or of Epiphany is a strong visual tie to our earliest

tradition, when the infancy narratives were written down. Such liturgical symbols permit us to reflect on the impact of the story through the centuries, and to be curious about the influence it might have on the future, possibly through our own doing or lack of it.

Turning the Advent wreath into a *Christmas wreath* by inserting a Christ candle into the center and by changing the ribbons to a festive red or royal blue, or gold, symbolizes the same inner posture: he was desired for ages, his coming was a historical event, and now we maintain a spirit of joyful hope until he comes again.

The strongest symbol in our region is the *Christmas tree.* To make it appear fresh and new and appealing each year, we may want to change its position within the church from time to time and alter its decoration. Its traditional meaning, though, remains as strong today as when it was first introduced: a joyful tree of life, the shiny ornaments symbolizing Jesus, the fruit of our desire, as well as the good deeds and graces which a life of his people comprises.

In one church I saw several beautiful trees placed in the middle aisle at even distances. One held a number of red apples, celebrating paradise, and tracing back Christ's mission to the very root of Adam and Eve's sin. Another was adorned with a multitude of God's Eye symbols, showing God's early revelation to Abraham and Moses. The next one bore crosses, to rejoice in Christ's saving death and resurrection. Close to the nativity scene in the front was a splendid tree decorated with an array of traditional treasures and shiny lights, while on the other side of the crèche stood a beautiful bare tree—a question to us about the future of Christ and our own future. All parishioners had been involved in providing the ornaments. At one time or another during the preparation they were seriously faced with questions of waiting and promise, of sin and birth, of death and resurrection and of life in his kingdom, gained for us through the birth of the Son. What a splendid Christmas!

The Christian Home

If "protecting" the tradition becomes part of the planners' task, then we should widen our planning grounds and include the homes of our parishioners. With so many mothers working, there is hardly time and even less leisure to let Advent happen. It takes a real effort. But with our encouragement and reminders in the parish bulletin, and short explanations of the religious significance, some of the fine and simple deliberate actions may survive.

Counting the days till Christmas with the aid of an "Advent house" is a custom worth protecting, so is letting our children fill the crib with pieces of straw which represent their good deeds. St. Nicholas' Day could be remembered by putting small surprises in the children's shoes during the night. The

ritual of lighting a candle on the feast of St. Lucy in front of an image of the Blessed Virgin and asking for protection of young girls and women is as beautiful as placing a single rose before the picture of Our Lady of Guadalupe on December 12, the day of her appearance in Mexico. The blessing of homes on Epiphany gathers the entire household to welcome the presence of God-with-us.

Once we understand that the home too is a place for Advent-Christmas ritual, we will not invite our people to participate frequently in church activities, without, at the same time, honoring their desire and their ability to create ritual and stories on their own and in their own homes. Let us assist them in the simple use of the Advent wreath by printing in the parish bulletin a few *brief* prayers and a song which can be used at supper time when the candles are being lit. Some parishes provide, at a nominal cost, inexpensive candles and simple greens on the days before Advent, so that everybody can be prepared and begin in the beginning. (Don't go into a tizzy over purple and pink candles. This only distracts from the essentials and looks ugly in most homes anyhow. A sprig of evergreen or a wreath, the light, and praying together, that's what sanctifies a home, not a fancy construction that is not allowed to be lit and is never invited to bloom into a symbol of communal prayer.)

In a healthy community, Advent-Christmastime at home and Advent-Christmastime in public worship will support each other. Here is where the "metabolism" should be at work: let us not equate "keeping the seasons" solely with attending church services. The festive environment of these seasons belongs in our homes—with simple prayers, honest discussions and gatherings around the table—and in our church buildings—with the finest artistry and materials our communities can supply.

Gesture

Richard N. Fragomeni

The seasons of Advent and Christmas celebrate the great gestures of God's saving love—the forging of the kingdom among us. For this reason, the liturgical gestures of the assembly at this time of the year should manifest the wonder and depth of God's initial action of establishing the kingdom with people of flesh and blood, past, present and future.

Eugene A. Walsh, SS, noted liturgist and author, describes three basic gestures of the eucharistic assembly: gathering, listening and responding *(Gathering for Each Other,* Pastoral Arts Associates, 1981). These are the three most familiar gestures of human encounter. It is around these three actions, then, that parish liturgy planners can enhance the gestures of the liturgies of Advent and Christmas.

A word of caution, please! The liturgical renewal has run the course from endless innovation, many times for its own sake, to a counterreformation-like legalism that destroys the spirit of the rites. Balance is necessary! And that balance is achieved when we take the revised ritual books, in this case the sacramentary and the lectionary, and breathe life into these already sound structures. Like God bringing to life the dry bones in the valley of Ezekiel's vision, liturgy planners bring life to the rituals of the community by doing them well and with spirit. No more endless innovation is necessary. Therefore, rather than giving the reader clever new ideas, this essay comes as a way of encouraging parishes to do the familiar gestures of the liturgy with style and finesse during Advent and Christmas. And what more can be asked? Does not God use style and finesse when he continues the gestures of the kingdom among us? All we really do is imitate the age-old divine style of the Word dwelling among us.

The Gathering Gesture

Each Sunday, Christians gather for better or worse. The Advent-Christmas season is an important time to bring the gathering gestures of the parish into light—with the accent on *better.* People feel rushed at this season; parishes can make them feel at home. Many visitors and people who come to church only on holidays enter our assembly halls. The first gesture they experience, if of welcome and courtesy, might be enough to invite them to come back and stay for the rest of the year. To accomplish this gesture of welcoming, parish liturgy teams can ask themselves questions like these:

- Are we actively training and recruiting ministers of hospitality?
- Do these ministers do more than wear badges and take up the collection?
- Does the whole assembly know their role of welcoming each other and making room for one another?

The ministry of welcoming is important for the parish community all year long. The holiday season, when people are more open to each other, can certainly be the right moment to build habits of hospitality. During this time when we remember that God took a name with us, it is too bad that people are so nameless at our gatherings. Good welcoming gestures can change this anonymity into hospitality.

Processions are other gestures that bring the community together; like slow-moving dances they add an aura of dignity and purpose to the gathering. All year long our entrance processions move worshipers from a time filled with the preoccupations of business and housekeeping *(kronos)* to the meaningful presence of the kingdom with us *(kairos).* During Advent, accompanied by the music of the litanies or the familiar hymns of the assembly, processions lead the worshipers into a centering experience of the presence of God. At all costs, then, processions should be done with care. No pushing or shoving, or breathing down one another's necks is allowed. Aidan Kavanagh in his recent book, *Elements of Rite: A Handbook of Liturgical Style* (Pueblo Publishing Company, 1982), has this to say:

> The problem with many liturgical ministers is not that their bodies say too little but that they say too much and say it badly. In processions ministers "march" in clots as though clinging to each other for comfort or support rather than spacing themselves well so that their movement takes on a modest significance. A procession is a parade, not a bus queue. Liturgical body language is an art of great understatement, and as such requires physical discipline. The marks of the chisel should never show. (69)

The Advent wreath provides another gesture of gathering. Many parishes in the United States use the Advent wreath to mark the four Sundays of the season. Parish planners can ask themselves: How do the wreath and the gesture of lighting its candles enhance the total gathering rite? Some liturgists wonder if it further clutters the already "cluttered vestibule" of the gathering rites. To simplify the gathering rites, then, parishes have found it helpful to carry the lighted candles of the wreath in the gathering procession and simply put them in place. No formal lighting is then done. Regardless of the ceremonies around the Advent wreath, a commitment to the gestures of gathering well done is necessary.

Christmastime offers plenty of ways to use processions as gestures of gathering. Use all the aisles, carry tall candles, create the space of worship with worthy banners for the feast. Parish liturgy teams can begin early to create long banners to be carried in at the solemn Masses of Christmas. Tall banners carried in procession let the entire assembly know where the parade is, and where it is going. Banners that loom above the heads of the assembly, brightly colored and accented with bells can make the gathering procession of Christmas an elegant proclamation of God's epiphany.

A word can be said about the use of incense at the gathering rites and at the other appropriate times of the celebration. Good incense is expensive. The incense that is available at many religious goods stores is more sawdust than actual incense. Parishes should invest in quality incense at this time of the year. (Very fine incense can be purchased from Holy

Transfiguration Monastery, 278 Warren Street, Brookline MA 02146. Write for their catalog.) If parishes wish to use incense they should use clouds of it. (My Byzantine friends say that we should be able to see the cherubim and seraphim in it—clever for Christmas.) It we use this gesture, the nose must be able to respond to it well. The way a censer is handled by a presider, thurifer or deacon can speak either dignity or doom. Usually a lightweight censer with many openings is the best. (A parish may wish to invest in a Byzantine censer that has bells on it.) This gesture of swinging with the smoke, the smell (and the sound of bells) can enhance the assembly's gathering. If the incense is of fine quality, hardly anyone complains and many rejoice.

At Advent-Christmastime and always, the apex of the gathering gesture is the initial greeting and prayer of the assembly. With arms wide open and with much enthusiasm, the presider greets the assembly and for the first time the dialogue is signaled. The way we gather sets the tone for the other gestures of the celebration.

The Gestures of Listening

The gestures of listening are both active and passive. Proclaiming the scriptures well and the shared silence of a parish community are the focal points of these gestures.

The first gesture of listening that can be enhanced during these seasons is simply waiting for the assembly to be seated and still before any proclamation begins. This sounds elementary but it is important. An invitation by the presider "to sit at the edge of your seat" may portray and ask the body to respond to the urgency of the kingdom proclaimed in the word of God. Liturgy planners may engage in a study of *Lectionary for Mass: Introduction* (United States Catholic Conference, 1982) for their Advent preparation as a way to discover other gestures for improving the assembly's manner of listening.

One gesture, however, must be discussed here. Our notion of gesture often refers to something active. Yet, during the liturgy of the word, listening, a passive gesture, is most full in silence. The use of silence after the first two readings and the homily can lead an assembly during Advent and Christmas to a wonderful experience of the real presence of God in his word.

This is simply done. First, the assembly needs to be alerted to being attentive to the word. Slowly, perhaps each week of Advent, a few more moments of silence may be added after each reading for the communal savoring of God's word. The reader might remain at the ambo when the reading is finished. No movement, no functions like seating people take place at this time (or any time between the opening prayer and a pause between the gospel and the homily). Enjoy the richness of the silence—a half minute—maybe even a minute when the assembly gets comfortable with this gesture. Advent and Christmas celebrate the silence of the night when the word of God leaps into our hearts. Parish liturgy planners could certainly assist our community prayer at Sunday eucharist by offering an honest catechesis and experience of silence at this time.

The gestures at the gospel procession need to be examined as well. The sacramentary asks us to place a gospel book on the altar during the entrance procession. During the gospel acclamation it is taken by the deacon and carried in procession to the ambo. Following the silence after the second reading, the deacon gets the gospel book and, with solemnity of banners and incense and communal song, brings the book up to the reading place to proclaim the scripture passage. This type of "parade" should be rehearsed well by both ministers and musicians. The excitement of such a procession, this emphasis on the gospel proclamation, especially at Christmas and Epiphany, can stay deeply in the consciousness of the parish.

Lastly, on Christmas Day (as well as on March 25, the solemnity of the annunciation of the Lord) the sacramentary asks that at the profession of faith the assembly genuflect at the words "and became man." This gesture is commonly overlooked. A simple genuflection may not be enough here. Perhaps the posture of standing could be changed to kneeling and a moment of silence could be shared. Or more simply, a moment of silence could be shared without a change of posture. In any case, the people need to be reminded beforehand of the gesture since it is no longer in general usage.

The Gestures of Responding

The gestures of responding to God's word are two: first, the liturgical response in the eucharistic prayer and the communion rite; second, the social response in the gestures of justice and peace in our everyday transactions.

Parishes can certainly enhance the quality of the eucharistic prayers during Advent and Christmas by taking a look at the responses of the assembly within it. The questions planners can ask in this regard deal with the three acclamations of the assembly. Does the community really respond? Are the Holy, memorial acclamation and amen sung with lots of energy? It seems that the enthusiasm with which a community prays this prayer becomes a sign of the level of conversion of the group. Lifeless response within the building probably indicates lifeless response outside.

Since the presider has most of the lines during the eucharistic prayer, a parish liturgy team may extend a Christmas gesture of support to their presiders by giving genuine feedback to them about their presidential style. Perhaps a gift certificate for some voice lessons or vocal coaching, or a good book on presiding *(Strong, Loving and Wise* by Robert Hovda) could be a gesture of parish support.

Advent and Christmas may certainly awaken a sensitivity to the use of all nine eucharistic prayers. Many Sunday gatherings pray only the second or third eucharistic prayer. The three prayers for children (this is really a misnomer—these three prayers are excellent for adults as well) may be used. These prayers offer a variety of response-gestures for the assembly. In any case, a good look at the eucharistic prayer is called for: how it is proclaimed and how the assembly responds to it.

During these kingdom seasons bodily gesture during the Lord's Prayer can be appropriately enhanced. Advent and Christmas invite us to be open to the kingdom in our midst and share it for the life of the world. Presiders may well celebrate this openness by inviting the assembly to pray the Lord's Prayer with hands and arms upraised—the *orans* posture of the early church. This ancient gesture of prayer brings the whole person into response to the Father. Much too often our assemblies rush through the Lord's Prayer as if an automatic pilot was mistakenly set off; the prayer becomes rapid and its meaning blurred. The gesture of praying deliberately and purposefully communicates a great connection between persons and can lead the assembly to focus on openness to the kingdom. Keep the prayer slow, paced and well cadenced. Group prayer can come alive. Parishes can work at this before the celebration begins.

The social gestures by which we respond to God's word can best be described by a look at the Christmas story. In the Lucan account, when God wished to communicate to the Jewish shepherds about the birth of Jesus, he sent angels as the bearers of the good news. Jewish shepherds could relate to angels. And so, the shepherds came and saw and went home full of joy. Similarly, in Matthew's account the astrologers are enchanted by the invitation of a star. Certainly astrologers could relate to a star. And so, they also came and saw, and returned home changed.

During Advent and Christmas, Christians are still touched by the gestures of God, and they in turn come and see and return home. They return home to speak the language and the gestures that people comprehend today. Not stars and angels, but human gestures of compassion, peace and justice manifest that light has been born and has overcome the demons of the night. Gestures of reaching out to the poor, desolate and fearful people of our world is what *"Ite missa est"* is really about.

During these seasons, when our hearts turn to the presence of the kingdom and God's saving gestures, it is good for us to gather well and listen and respond with all the energy we can muster up—always remembering that it is God who invites us first. God's gestures become our own.

Music

Michael Joncas

For a pastoral musician the Advent-Christmas season presents unique opportunities and tensions. Opportunities for congregational singing abound, and even the most Scrooge-like character has been known to melt and join the refrain of *"Adeste fideles."* Carols in arrangements from the Mormon Tabernacle Choir to Alvin and the Chipmunks haunt our airwaves. Rare is the parent who will not hear little Jimmy or Janey serenading "Rudolph the red-nosed reindeer" or "Frosty the snowman." During this season the culture as a whole supports music-making as a sign of our common winter festivity.

But this same cultural support also creates tensions. First of all, Christmas carols appear in the secular media sometime around Thanksgiving and disappear immediately after December 25. In that sonic environment it is difficult to create a mood of longing and expectation appropriate to Advent or to prolong the joys of Christmas through the twelve days, let alone the Baptism of the Lord. Second, the barrage of traditional Christmas songs in dentists' offices and shopping malls can make their use in the Christian assembly anti-climactic. Pastoral musicians are faced with the expectation in their congregations for the kind of polished sounds possible on record or tape but impossible in communal song. The unspoken assumption is that we bring out the "best" for Christmas—brass groups, recorder consorts, well-rehearsed choirs—but this very instinct for musical elaboration can subtly invite the assembly to be entertained by visiting professionals rather than to engage in common faith-song. Third, while many of the texts of our Christmas songs are genuine folk expressions of the wonder of the incarnation, many others are vague paeans to sentiment and goodwill. There is little of the bracing realism of the Christian gospel that connects the child of Bethlehem with the man of sorrows, that yokes the enfleshment of God with the dead-and-living one. Finally, the pastoral musician who desires to enrich the assembly's prayer with new musical repertoire faces an often recalcitrant assembly with little inclination for music rehearsal and a significant number of congregants whose only foray into common worship happens during this season.

The pastoral musician can capitalize on the opportunities and minimize the tensions of the Advent-Christmas season. The use of hymns and carols, psalmody and canticles, acclamations and litanies in eucharistic liturgy throughout this time can create an aural environment to mark these days of wonder and fulfillment.

Hymns and Carols

There is a vast repertoire of Advent and Christmastime hymns and carols. Pastoral musicians might begin their planning process by consulting the selections available in standard modern hymnals: #200–240 of the *Catholic Liturgy Book* (Helicon, 1975); the Advent, Christmas and Epiphany indexes of *Worship II* (GIA, 1975) and the *Catholic Book of Worship II* (Canadian Conference of Catholic Bishops, 1980); and #22–90 as well as the supplementary indexes of the *Lutheran Book of Worship* (Augsburg, 1978). In addition, the classic collections of the Episcopal *Hymnal* (1940) and the *Oxford Book of Carols* should be consulted.

I recommend that pastoral musicians search out both "hymns of the season" and "hymns of the day." A hymn of the season (e.g., "O come, O come, Emmanuel" or "Come, thou long-expected Jesus" during Advent; "O come, all ye faithful" or "Joy to the world" during Christmastime) can be sung throughout the season without conflicting with the shifting focuses the scriptures offer and without boredom in the assembly. Relying on these hymns year after year can give continuity to the assembly's experience of the season, creating a comfort level that allows the assembly to enter into the ritual prayer without much self-consciousness. Often hymns of the season function well as gathering or concluding songs. Their very familiarity challenges the pastoral musician to use a variety of verses and to expand the assembly's musical horizons by offering contrasts in congregational singing (divided men/women, right side/left side, solo/choir/all) or instrumental accompaniment on different verses.

The hymn of the day, in contrast, is designed to complement the unique scriptural proclamation of a festival's readings. I often employ the hymn of the day as a congregational anthem after the homily to confirm and personalize the preached message. Homilists may enrich and inform their spoken text with the evocative and poetic phrases of a well-chosen hymn. Normally the hymn of the day will directly comment on the gospel reading, but it may also be used to point up aspects of the other readings not touched upon in the homily. The sample program that follows is not meant for imitation, but to spark your own creativity in discovering hymnic expansion of the proclaimed word. Note how each of these hymn texts furthers the gospel of the day in each of the three cycles of the Sunday lectionary.

Advent I "The King shall come when morning dawns" (W II, #269)
The King shall come when morning dawns
And light and beauty brings.
Hail, Christ the Lord! Thy people pray:
"Come quickly, King of Kings!"

Advent II "On Jordan's bank" (CBW II, #443)
On Jordan's bank the Baptist's cry
Announces that the Lord is nigh;
Awake and hearken for he brings
Glad tidings of the King of Kings.

Advent III "Comfort, comfort now my people" (LBW, #29)
For the herald's voice is crying
In the desert far and near
Calling us to true repentance
Since the Kingdom now is here.

Oh, that warning cry obey!
Now for God prepare a way!
Let the valleys rise to meet him,
And the hills bow down to greet him!

Advent IV

"Praise we the Lord this day"
(W II, #232)
She meekly bowed her head
To hear the gracious word,
Mary the pure and lowly maid
The favored of the Lord.
Blessed shall be her name
In all the church on earth
Through whom that wondrous mercy came
Th'incarnate Savior's birth.

Christmas

"A stable lamp is lighted"
(LBW, #74)
But now as at the ending
The low is lifted high;
The stars shall bend their voices
And every stone shall cry.
And every stone shall cry
In praises of the Child
By whose descent among us
The worlds are reconciled.

Holy Family

"Our Father, by whose name"
(LBW, #357)
Our Father, by whose name
All parenthood is known:
In love divine you claim
Each family as your own. . . .

Mary, Mother of God

"The God whom earth and sea and sky"
(W II, #265)
O Mother blest! the chosen shrine
Wherein the Architect divine
Whose hand contains the earth and sky
Vouchsafed in hidden guise to lie:
Blest in the message Gabriel brought
Blest in the work the Spirit wrought;
Most blest, to bring to human birth
The long desired of all the earth.

Epiphany "As with gladness men of old" (CLB, #234)

As with gladness men of old
Did the guiding star behold;
As with joy they hailed its light
Leading onward, beaming bright;
So, most gracious Lord, may we
Evermore be led to thee.

Baptism of the Lord "When Jesus comes to be baptized" (CBW II, #480)

The Spirit of the Lord comes down,
Anoints the Christ to suffering,
To preach the word, to free the bound
And to the mourner, comfort bring.

Finally, many communities have a custom of singing carols for an extended period of time before the Christmas Midnight Mass; such singing serves well as an assembly-based gathering rite. Perhaps carol-singing by the assembly might be encouraged before and after the eucharist throughout Christmastime. In addition, all parish meetings through the season could begin and end with a verse of a simple carol. Families could be encouraged to carol in their neighborhoods during the twelve days, and to sing a gentle Christmas lullaby as a wonderful bedtime prayer.

Psalmody and Canticles

The lectionary offers both proper and common responsorial psalms for Advent and Christmastime. My pastoral experience suggests that communities, especially those without many musical resources, would be well advised to choose a single Advent psalm and one Christmastime psalm for use throughout the respective seasons. The longing for fulfillment and visionary character of Advent are well captured in the appointed common psalms. Psalm 25 with its refrain, "To you, O Lord, I lift up my soul," speaks of learning the ways of the Lord, the paths of his truth, and with humility being guided to his justice. This dream of the "peaceable kingdom" is vividly sketched in Psalm 85 with its refrain, "Lord, let us see your kindness": "Kindness and truth shall meet / justice and peace shall kiss." Musical settings for these texts should be simple and artless, with spare instrumentation and gentle harmonizations. Perhaps the Advent psalm could be sung a cappella or accompanied by a single wind instrument (e.g., recorder, oboe, flute); adaptations of the Gregorian chant formulas would be appropriate.

In contrast, the common psalms for Christmas and Epiphany are outgoing and expansive. Psalm 98 with its refrain, "All the ends of the earth have seen the saving power of God," jubilantly hymns the *mirabilia Dei* in unbounded rejoicing, calling on all the voices and instruments of humankind to sing God's victory. Psalm 72 with its refrain, "Lord, every nation on earth shall adore you," is problematic. The text was clearly chosen for its reference to "kings of the earth bearing tribute," yet the earlier verses begging God to provide a just "king" and "king's son" may seem at best quaint to contemporary ears. Nonetheless, the desire for equitable governance is very much a contemporary theme. Perhaps the problem can be avoided by having Psalm 98 function throughout the season, including the festivals of Epiphany and Baptism of the Lord. If Psalm 72 is used, the preacher may want to make reference to its typological use. The Christmastime psalm calls for rich instrumentation and strong rhythms; peals of bells and brass fanfares would not be inappropriate.

The singing of scriptural canticles can also enrich the musical prayer of Advent-Christmastime. *The Book of Canticles* (The Church Hymnal Corporation, 1979) is a wonderful initial resource for developing canticle singing. The texts are set to plainsong adapted from Gregorian and Sarum chants, contemporary chant, and various formulas of Anglican chant. Texts especially appropriate to Advent include the three "Songs of Isaiah" *(Ecce Deus* [Is 12:2–6]; *Quaerite Dominum* [Is 55:6–11]; and *Surge, illuminare* [Is 60:1–3, 11a, 14c, 18–19]). During Christmastime appropriate canticles include the *Gloria in excelsis* and the *Te Deum laudamus.* Of course both the *Benedictus* (Lk 1:68–79) and the *Magnificat* (Lk 1:46–55), (especially in a metrical hymnic setting) could be used in both Advent and Christmastime. Although canticle singing has traditionally been associated more with the liturgy of the hours, canticles might be employed at eucharist as gathering or concluding music, anthems during the preparation of gifts and altar, or postcommunion thanksgivings.

Acclamations and Litanies

The great acclamatory plea of the Advent season is *maranatha,* an Aramaic phrase variously translated as "The Lord is coming!" or "Come soon, Lord!" Three settings that employ this ancient liturgical cry come from the *Music from Taizé* collection (GIA, 1981). "Maranatha—Alleluia II" could serve as a strong gospel acclamation, while "Maranatha—*Veni Domine"* would function well as a repeated refrain after sung general intercessions. The double canon *"Ostende nobis"* is a magnificent ritual processional with a Latin text translated "Lord, show us your mercy. Amen! Come soon!" In keeping with the character of the season, I would again recommend that these acclamations be sung a cappella or with very sparse wind instrument accompaniment. In *Trocaire* (Cooperative Music, 1982) Christopher Willcock, SJ, has produced two fine acclamatory pieces for Advent. In "The Spirit of the Lord" he has adapted the text of Isaiah 61 as an extended gospel acclamation for soloist, choir and assembly. His setting of eucharistic prayer II includes a chant line for the presider and a wonderful doxology/amen based on the melody *Veni, veni, Emmanuel.*

The corresponding acclamation for the Christmas season is most probably the *Gloria in excelsis Deo* from the angelic hymn in the gospel of Luke. *Music from Taizé* includes three canonic settings of this text that could serve well as gospel acclamations, communion processionals, or chant *ostinato* "backgrounds" to the proclamation of the eucharistic prayer. The refrain of "Angels we have heard on high" might also be employed as an acclamation before and after the gospel reading. These Christmastime acclamations demand bright instrumentation (brass, bells, decorative strings and/or woodwinds), enthusiastic singing by the assembly, and "layered" harmonization by a choir/schola.

A troped setting of the Lamb of God could be employed at the fraction rite; various Advent (Key of David, Morning Star, Root of Jesse) and Christmastime (God-Hero, Wonder-Counselor, Prince of Peace) titles of the Lord could be employed to the same melodies to mark the change of the season.

Once the pastoral musician has an organized idea of the musical program for the Advent-Christmastime eucharists, attention can shift to the liturgy of hours, reconciliation services, festivals of lessons and carols, etc. Perhaps the most important imaginative principle is to try to create an aural environment of longing and dreaming during Advent (imagine distant wind chimes in a winter storm) and gutsy festivity during Christmastime (the Salvation Army street-corner band or neighbors caroling with mugs of cider before a roaring fire).

APPENDIX A

Preaching in Advent: Rethinking the Fulfillment Theme

John T. Pawlikowski, OSM

In the Advent season, with its extensive use of readings from the prophets, the potential for the denigration of Judaism is real though subtle.

Promises and Preludes?

The readings from the prophets selected for the three cycles appear to push the hearers of the word in one common direction—the Jesus whose coming we celebrate at Christmas is the fulfillment of the message of hope and promise they proclaimed. Under this line of thinking, Jesus' birth is viewed as the inauguration of the "days to come" spoken of by Isaiah in A cycle and Jeremiah in the C cycle.

Sections of these readings can easily leave the impression that pre-Jesus Israel was guilt-ridden and in mourning, eagerly awaiting its liberation. We listen on the Second Sunday of Advent (C cycle) to Baruch's summons to Jerusalem to "take off your robe of mourning and misery," or in the B cycle to Isaiah speaking about the anticipated, imminent expiation of Jerusalem's guilt. It is very difficult for the average Catholic worshiper, conditioned for so long by stereotypes of Judaism's spiritual vapidity and notions of Jewish suffering as punishment, not to imagine that Jesus' coming marked the liberation of people from the emptiness and sinfulness of Judaism.

When Isaiah in cycle A complains about the house of David "wearying" God himself, when Zephaniah in year C tells us that the Lord has removed the judgment against Jerusalem, and when Isaiah again (at Midnight Mass) speaks of the people "who walked in darkness," this sense of overriding Jewish guilt intensifies. The impression can easily be drawn from these readings, and often is by homilists, that Judaism was incapable of any spiritual regeneration short of the emergence of the messiah who is clearly identified with Jesus.

The way the readings have been selected and arranged can also lead us to believe that the prophets clearly foresaw the details of Jesus' birth and that their words were primarily directed to this event. On the Fourth Sunday of Advent in year C we hear Micah speak of the ruler of Israel coming from Bethlehem-Ephrathah. And there are references in the readings of all the cycles to King David and to a virgin giving birth. The subtle message seems to be that anyone who knew the Hebrew Scriptures ought to have recognized Jesus as the expected Jewish messiah.

Advent preachers confront a basic problem here. The implied exegesis of these prophetic texts as they have been set up by the framers of the liturgy stands in tension with what many biblical theologians and writers on Christology are saying. Leading scripture scholars have clearly repudiated the notion that the prophets in these readings were expressly speaking about the birth of Jesus. John L. McKenzie is one who has made this point in decisive language:

> This writer has said elsewhere that Jesus is the Messiah of Judaism, and that he can be understood only as Messiah of Judaism. I stand by this observation, but I do not believe that it obliges me to find faith in Jesus Messiah in the Old Testament. Jesus transformed the idea of Messiah when he fulfilled it. The total reality of Jesus Messiah is found nowhere in the Old Testament, not even in its totality. (*A Theology of the Old Testament*, 31–32).

The misguided interpretations of the prophets as directly foretelling the coming of Christ is really part of a general Christian misuse of the Hebrew Scriptures. We in the church have tended to look on the Hebrew Scriptures only as prelude, only as giving us glimpses of the New Testament message. We have generally failed to appreciate its spiritual richness in its own right. There exists a mandate for Catholics to move away from this narrow approach to the Hebrew Scriptures which not only leads to negative portrayals of Judaism but hampers our own spiritual development. This direction is clear from the recent words of Pope John Paul II. Speaking to the Jewish community at Mainz, West Germany, the Pope recalled a statement of Vatican Council II. In its *Declaration on the Church and the Jewish People,* the council insisted that "the effort must be made to understand better everything in the Old Testament that has its own, permanent value . . . since this value is not wiped out by the later interpretations of the New Testament."

If we then examine most major works of systematic Christology today, we find that in their interpretations of the Christ-event there is little reliance on the "fulfillment of Old Testament prophecies" motif that so dominates the Advent liturgy. The theologians are aware of the direction that scripture scholars have taken on the question.

The Prophet's Task

There are definite possibilities for preaching on the Advent texts that will lessen their anti-Semitic potential. First of all, emphasis should be placed on the fact that the prophets were speaking first and foremost to the people of their own day. Their concern was not to foretell the future nor to announce the advent of Christ. Speaking in the name of God, the root meaning of the term "prophet," and with divine authority, they were reminding the people of their covenantal obligations. They realized that God and his people had become estranged through human unfaithfulness. They hoped to overcome the alienation by reminding people of the dire consequences if they ignored the message, but they also recalled that there could be a new fullness of divine help if the people would turn away from their sin.

Jewish and Christian Responses

The second point we need to emphasize is that an adequate response to the prophetic call was not totally delayed until the coming of Jesus. The rebuilding of the Temple and the rapid growth of the Pharisaic movement during the Second Temple (or intertestamental) period clearly illustrate the seriousness with which the people Israel took the prophets' warnings. They knew they had endured exile as a punishment for unfaithfulness. Following the lead of the prophets, many were determined that this painful experience would never be repeated.

The period in which Jesus was born and preached was not one in which Judaism was spiritually bankrupt. *Some* Jews hoped for a political messiah who would liberate them from the political oppression of the Roman conquerors of Palestine. Others, like the Pharisees, turned their attention to the total rebuilding of the daily life and spirit of the Jewish people. Jesus was part of this effort, though he had some distinctive ideas not widely shared by other Jews. (I develop this in *Christ in Light of the Christian-Jewish Dialogue,* published by Paulist Press.)

The Second Temple period was for both Judaism and the newly born Christian community a time when the prophetic promise of a new inrush of divine grace was being realized. It was not invalid for the gospel writers to speak of the coming of Jesus within the framework of traditional prophetic categories of judgment/promise. Jesus certainly represents in Christian eyes a new outpouring of divine help, the promise of human salvation. In his ministry and in his person the alienation between God and his people which so concerned the prophets was being overcome. But it would be just as legitimate to apply these words to the regeneration efforts under way in Judaism at the same time. While church and synagogue eventually found it necessary to go their separate ways, they both represented serious and constructive, though somewhat different, responses to the earlier call of the prophets for renewed faithfulness. Contrary to popular belief in the church, it was not only the Christian community which was responsive to the words of Isaiah, Jeremiah, Baruch and others.

Emmanuel

Third, preaching in Advent can and must emphasize the centrality of the incarnation. It is a unique doctrine developed from the preaching and ministry of Jesus, even though there already existed in Second Temple Judaism a growing sense of God's intimacy with humanity. But belief in the incarnation does not automatically invalidate the continuing meaningfulness of Judaism. However theologians may eventually restate the theological relationship between the two faith communities (a process that is still in its infancy), the basic point remains that from a Christian perspective both traditions retain a central value. This view has been clearly affirmed by the Vatican Council and by the recent popes.

Christianity considers God's intervention in Christ to be decisive, but (and this must be stressed) this intervention did not represent the coming of the messianic kingdom in the Jewish sense. This is the point made by McKenzie. If Jesus is the messiah, it is in a transformed sense and hence Judaism was not "blind" in not recognizing a connection between Jesus and the messianic kingdom. Increasingly Christian theology has placed strong emphasis on the "not yet" dimension of the Christ-event. The messianic kingdom for both Jews and Christians still lies ahead. As we wait together, as we work together, the prophetic selections read during Advent can become a new summons to the church to reach out to the Jewish people and recognize them as partners in the building of the kingdom.

Such cooperation is especially timely with respect to the imperative of justice. Though this theme is highlighted more in the readings from Isaiah used in the A cycle, there is no reason why it cannot be raised in other years as a way of urging Catholics to join Jews in a common response to this prophetic call. Pope John Paul II spoke directly to this in his German address: "Jews and Christians, as children of Abraham, are called to be a blessing for the world (cf. Gn 12:2ff) by committing themselves together for peace and justice among all persons and peoples."

Since from the Christian perspective both Jews and Christians share in the covenantal relationship with God (cf. Rom 11:29), only by working together can we bring about the full realization of the final messianic kingdom. This should be made clear in our preaching this Advent. Jews are not antagonists, but partners, in the messianic dream we celebrate during the Advent-Christmas season.

APPENDIX B

A Merry Christmas Bulletin

Ron Lewinski

Christmas is homecoming season. Parish Christmas Masses are filled to the brim with college students home on break, out-of-town guests and relatives of parishioners, old parishioners back for a friendly visit, the not-so-active Catholics reaffirming their roots, and of course the faithful who are there every week. This homecoming time is an opportunity to make good use of the parish bulletin. Even when Christmas is not on a Sunday, a special edition could serve as a warm introduction to the parish for newcomers or infrequent worshipers. If printed handsomely and offered kindly, this bulletin can be a take-home gift that will remind of the parish and the Christmas celebration.

What might this special edition of the parish bulletin contain? First of all, it ought to include a warm welcome from the pastor and staff. This is not the time to chastise the infrequent worshipers but to genuinely welcome them. College students deserve a special word of welcome so they will know we are truly happy to have them back home at worship.

Include an overview of the parish's life in this bulletin: not a drab listing of items but a sketch of the whole. Catch the spirit and vision of the parish. Use pictures and write about the people, not just the programs and policies. A photo and brief biographies of the pastoral staff might be appreciated. Be conscious of all age levels and be sensitive to invalids who may be receiving the bulletin at home or in the hospital from family or ministers of care.

The Christmas feast naturally draws the unchurched and members of other Christian communions to worship with family or neighbors. It becomes, therefore, a good occasion to acquaint people with the catechumenate. Give them an idea of what the Christian initiation of adults involves. They may be waiting for an invitation like this.

Many Catholics may be present who have drifted back to the church after years of nonpractice. Offer them an opportunity to return for some prayer, counsel, dialogue and updating (perhaps in a process similar to the RCIA).

The general plan and dates for the parish's observance of Lent might be ready for announcement at Christmas. Invite the Christmas congregation to set aside the lenten dates now.

Some of those attending at Christmas may be new to the area. Welcome them and inform them how they can easily go about registering as parishioners.

If there is another parish that is a "twin" (where each helps the other), include some general information and pictures from the twin parish. This shows the broader concerns of the parish.

The special Christmas edition of the bulletin can be given by Catholics to their neighbors and friends. A great deal about a parish can be caught from the tone of the bulletin. In addition to the items above, include some Christmas prayers and family Christmas customs. In particular a service of prayer for the family Christmas table and a model of prayer to be used around the Christmas tree or crèche would be welcome and useful at home. There could also be suggestions on observing the rest of the Christmas season. If you plan ahead, invite parishioners to share their own family traditions and print these in the bulletin.

The special Christmas bulletin is a gift. The cost is relatively small and ordinarily can be assumed by regular bulletin advertisers. It may be a few pages longer, but the effort will be well spent.

The good response to a special Merry Christmas bulletin will make it a parish Christmas tradition.

We warmly welcome all who have come today to celebrate this glorious feast.
We welcome the stranger, the traveller and guest!
We welcome our students home from college for a good winter's rest!
We welcome parishioners who moved far away
but join us today as old friends and guests!
We welcome all who have not been active of late in their Catholic faith;
and hope they will find new hope and inspiration this Christmas to come back again and again!
We welcome our faithful parishioners, loyal and true;
may the Lord bless you for all you do!
Welcome to all! May our gathering this day gladden our hearts
and deepen our bonds.
We are after all one People of God—redeemed by the Light.
May we walk by the Light and live by the Light—together in love.

CHRISTMAS BLESSINGS!

APPENDIX C

Epiphany and the Gift of Time

Robert H. Oldershaw

Extending the celebration of Christmas beyond December 25 is an annual challenge for liturgy planners. Here's an idea (tried in one parish) that may help the Christmas celebration build to Epiphany by the simple enrichment of a custom already present in many parishes: the annual distribution of calendars.

Ordinarily, a week or two before New Year's, ushers distribute calendars imprinted with parish information to the people as they leave Mass. It's a fairly perfunctory gesture. The suggestion is to turn this simple distribution into the giving of a gift.

First of all, give the calendars on Epiphany. During the days before, invite some children or adults of the parish to gift wrap them. One simple way is to tie a bow on each calendar. Tying the ribbon through the nail-hanging hole enables people to hang the calendar without removing the ribbon—thus providing a constant reminder of the gift of time! This works better than rolling the calendar like a scroll, especially if they are the Extension Society calendars which are awkward to roll.

Give the parish advance notice that the calendars will be distributed on Epiphany (the people won't think you've forgotten to order them).

The liturgy should focus on the gift of time. The revelation of the Lord to the world happens in our time—this year, in and through this parish—as we experience together once again the saving mystery of Christ. This is the rhythm of the year of grace: Lent-Easter with its special moments (Ash Wednesday, the Three Days, Ascension, Pentecost) the beat of Ordinary Time culminating in the feast of Christ the King, and once again awaiting the advent of the Lord. The homily could reflect on this and lead to the "Epiphany proclamation"—an ancient tradition of announcing the movable feasts of the year on the feast of Epiphany after the proclamation of the gospel. (A musical setting of the Epiphany proclamation is usually included in the November/December issue of *Liturgy 80* [LTP].)

Before beginning the proclamation (which is sung by a cantor), the homilist speaks of the calendars which will be presented to the assembly as gifts of the parish—a sign of God's abiding presence in our time. Then the men and women who serve as ushers come forward. Half of them hold baskets or trays filled with the calendars. Holding these up for all to see, they stand beside the cantor. Before the proclamation is sung, the book holding the proclamation and all the calendars can be honored with incense. Then the cantor chants the proclamation.

Immediately after the chanting of the proclamation, the ushers, taking *time* and *care, present* the calendars to the assembly. The ushers work in teams, one holding a basket and the other passing out the calendars. This is an important moment for ushers who don't often have an opportunity to be bearers of gifts. Today they are the magi! It's essential that the significance of their role be well explained to them. A perfunctory distribution can spoil a lovely gesture.

This need not add significantly to the length of the liturgy. The spoken part of the homily might be brief, preparing for the action which, if carefully done, will speak more effectively than many words.

An afterthought for advance planning: a greeting or blessing might be imprinted on the calendar. "Presented on the feast of Epiphany, 19__." This imprinting is usually done by the calendar companies by spring or summer of the previous year.

Contributors

Richard N. Fragomeni is a priest of the diocese of Albany and coordinator of that diocese's liturgy center.

Michael Joncas is a composer and liturgist. He is currently associate pastor of the Church of the Presentation of the Blessed Virgin Mary in Maplewood, Minnesota.

Regina Kuehn, an artist and lecturer, is a frequent contributor to LTP's publications.

Eugene LaVerdiere, SSS, is a scripture scholar on the faculty of Chicago's Catholic Theological Union.

Ron Lewinski is a priest of the archdiocese of Chicago. He is associate pastor of St. Marcelline Parish in Schaumburg and director of the catechumenate for the archdiocese.

Robert H. Oldershaw, a priest of the archdiocese of Chicago, serves as associate director for music of Chicago's Office for Divine Worship and associate pastor of St. Clement Church, Chicago.

John T. Pawlikowski, OSM, is a member of the Catholic Bishops' Secretariat for Catholic-Jewish Relations and is on the faculty of Catholic Theological Union in Chicago.

Peter J. Scagnelli is associate pastor of Our Lady of Mt. Carmel Church in Bristol, Rhode Island.

Mary Ann Simcoe is a liturgist and editor at Liturgy Training Publications.